THE RAMAKIEN

THE

J. M. CADET

RAMAKIEN

THE THAI EPIC

*Illustrated with
the bas-reliefs of Wat Phra Jetubon,
Bangkok*

KODANSHA INTERNATIONAL LTD.,
Tokyo, Japan & Palo Alto, California, U.S.A.

Distributed in the British Commonwealth (excluding Canada
and the Far East) by Ward Lock & Company Ltd., London and
Sydney; in Continental Europe by Boxerbooks, Inc., Zurich;
and in the Far East by Japan Publications Trading Co., C.P.O.
Box 722, Tokyo. Published by Kodansha International Ltd.,
2–12–21, Otowa, Bunkyo-ku, Tokyo 112, Japan and Kodansha
International/USA, Ltd., 599 College Avenue, Palo Alto,
California 94306. Copyright © 1970, by Kodansha Inter-
national Ltd. All rights reserved. Printed in Japan.
  Library of Congress Catalogue Card No. 70–128685
  SBN 87011–134–5
  JBC 0098–782816–2361
First edition, 1971

CONTENTS

12.   11.   10.   9.   8.   7.

LIST OI

24.   23.   22.   21.   20.   19.

6.   5.   4.   3.   2.   1.

BAS-RELIEF PANELS

18.   17.   16.   15.   14.   13.

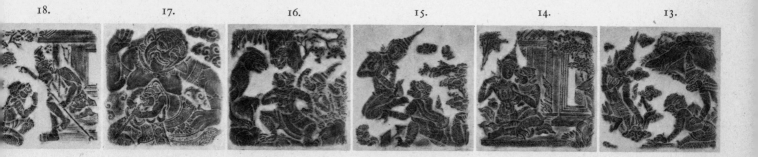

36.   35.   34.   33.   32.   31.

48.   47.   46.   45.   44.   43.

30.   29.   28.   27.   26.   25.

THE BANISHMENT OF PIPECK

42.   41.   40.   39.   38.   37.

60.   59.   58.   57.   56.   55.

72.   71.   70.   69.   68.   67.

54.   53.   52.   51.   50.   49.

66.   65.   64.   63.   62.   61.

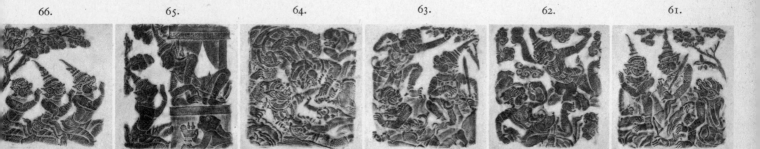

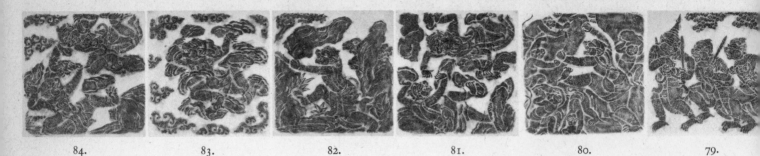

84.   83.   82.   81.   80.   79.

96.   95.   94.   93.   92.   91.

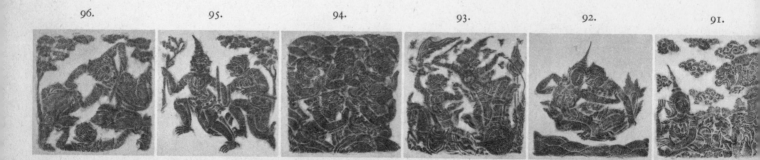

78.   77.   76.   75.   74.   73.

90.   89.   88.   87.   86.   85.

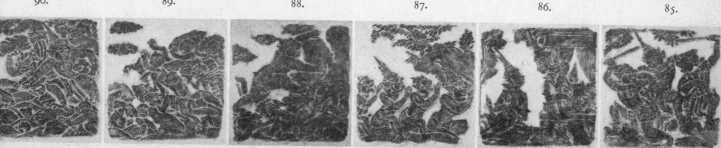

108.   107.   106.   105.   104.   103.

97. *Hanuman decapitates Panurat*

98. *Hanuman brings Panurat's head to Phra Ram*

99. *Phra Ram praises Hanuman*

100. *Ongkot confronts Totsagan*

101. *Four guards try to seize Ongot*

102. *Ongkot breaks down the palace gate*

103. *Totsagan's nephews ride to the underworld*

104. *Maiyarap, Lord of the Underworld, receives Totsagan's nephews*

105. *Maiyarap smashes his chariot*

106. *Maiyarap conducts magic rites*

107. *Maiyarap enters the sleeping Hanuman's mouth*

108. *Maiyarap flies to the underworld with Phra Ram*

120.   119.   118.   117.   116.   115.

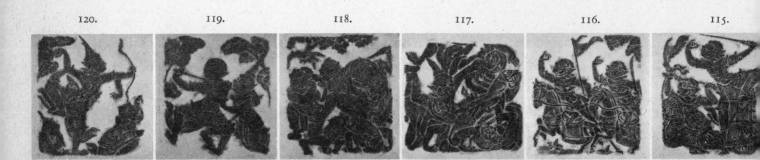

102.   101.   100.   99.   98.   97.

THE DEFEAT OF KUMPAGAN
AND INTORACHIT

114.   113.   112.   111.   110.   109.

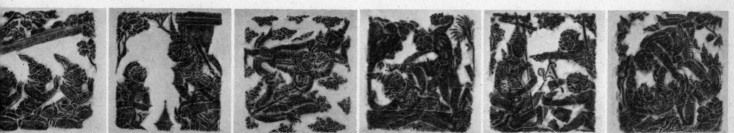

132. 131. 130. 129. 128. 127.

144. 143. 142. 141. 140. 139.

126.   125.   124.   123.   122.   121.

138.   137.   136.   135.   134.   133.

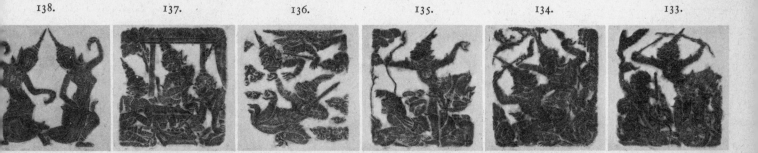

150.   149.   148.   147.   146.   145.

145. *Phra Ram and Phra Lak ride out to meet Sahatsadecha*

146. *Mounted on woodland beasts, the monkeys charge Mulplam*

147. *Phra Lak, aided by Hanuman, fights with Mulplam*

148. *Hanuman pulls the spear from Phra Lak's wound*

149. *Mounted on Hanuman's shoulders, Phra Lak shoots at Mulplam*

150. *Phra Lak's arrow kills Mulplam*

151. *Hanuman grapples with Sahatsadecha, who is trying to escape with his concubines*

152. *Hanuman kills Sahatsadecha*

152.   151.

NOTE AND ACKNOWLEDGEMENTS

Although the *Ramakien* provides the most important theme in Thai literature, it has yet to be translated directly into English. This version of the epic does not represent an attempt to remedy this deficiency. It is neither a translation—for which neither the Thai at my command nor the time at my disposal were sufficient—nor is it a summary, as it deals principally with the central episode of the story. It can best be described as a renarration of the *Ramakien* of King Rama I, based upon the bas-reliefs of Wat Phra Jetubon, and as such is as faithful to its sources as brevity permits. Although the Wat Phra Jetubon bas-reliefs deal only with the central episode of the story, I have added a prologue and epilogue so that the reader may see how the *Ramakien* begins and ends.

Facts of any description are hard to come by in Thailand. Conscious that without their help the information that I have been able to bring to light would have remained hidden, I wish to offer my thanks to: Koon Chucheep Thiarapongse-Boyle, Mrs. I. Eisenhofer, Koon Koolasap Gesmankit, Koon Sompop Jantrapan and Professor Kien Yimsiri.

Two persons without whose aid this work could not have come into being warrant particular mention: Charles Burleigh, from whose collection of rubbings the illustrations in this book are taken. And Koon Lakana Devaprateep, who guided my stumbling footsteps through the darkest thickets of the Thai language. To both my heartiest thanks.

J. M. CADET

INTRODUCTION

The Thai are one of the more elusive peoples of the Orient.

Although the West has been in constant contact with the Southeast Asian kingdom since the sixteenth century, and in spite of the glamor that has always invested the court and people of Siam (as the country was called until recently), the number of definitive or even reliably informative works on the Thai amounts to no more than a handful.

This is the more puzzling as few Asian countries are as accessible as Thailand, and few peoples more apparently friendly towards foreigners.   Neither political, religious nor social obstacles of an overt kind stand before the institutions, temples and homes of the Thai, and many Westerners, thinking that to see is to understand, gain the impression from having seen so much of the country and people that they understand it—and them—completely. But nothing could be further from the truth.   For like the chameleon, the Thai have perfected the useful art of being fully in view and remaining almost invisible.   And nowhere is this art better displayed than at the Bangkok temple of Phra Jetubon.*

If Thailand has an omphalos, it is here.   The temple stands on a tongue of land guarded by two canals and a wall, and here, at the center of the nucleus from which modern Bangkok grew, the ashes of the first king of the ruling dynasty repose.   Nothing prevents the visitor from entering this splendid royal mausoleum, nor from strolling through its spacious and serene courtyards, past huge gate guardians from China and stone lingams from India, between glittering reliquaries and through dim cloisters, to the central chapel.   No one prohibits him from approaching this chapel, the Phra Ubosot, or "Main Chapel," and inspecting its remarkable reliefs, nor from entering the building and standing before the Buddha that surmounts the royal ashes.   But it is here that he is brought to a standstill.   For while nowhere else—certainly not in most Hindu or Moslem communities—would he have been permitted to come so far, nowhere else will he find it so difficult to make any further progress.   Here he encounters the barrier with which the Thai protect themselves.

---

* Commonly called Wat Po, sometimes called Wat Potharam, but properly entitled Wat Phra Jetubon Weemol Mungklaram.

Even before this point the visitor will have been aware that certain natural and to some extent inevitable obstacles stand between himself and the people of the country. He will have discovered that Thailand, alone of all Southeast Asian countries, has never been the colony of a Western power, and that, perhaps as a result, few Thai speak English well, and not all that many speak it at all. This will naturally hamper his communication with the people, for his own attempts to speak Thai, a five-toned, more or less monosyllabic language related to Chinese, are unlikely to be understood. He will also have learned that in escaping the major mischiefs of colonization, Thailand also missed its minor benefits, among them the attentions of European scholars. The compendious works in European languages on the social and natural histories, the languages and customs, which one almost takes for granted in the newly independent countries of Asia, have no counterparts in Thailand. Furthermore, the visitor is unlikely to turn to Thai sources for information not available to him in English, for a written language of forty-four consonants and thirty-two vowels in a Sanscrit-type script is not to be mastered in a matter of weeks. But even if he does so, the visitor will be disappointed. For works of scholarship as they are known elsewhere—detailed, meticulously accurate, comprehensive in coverage and themselves rooted in a long tradition of independent inquiry—are not to be found in Thailand.

So even before arriving at the central reliquary of Wat Phra Jetubon, the visitor will have become aware of the obstacles that stand between himself and an even partial understanding of what he sees. But it is in attempting to go beyond the point at which he has been halted that he encounters the final and decisive barrier. For in consulting the monks of the temple, curators of museums, university dons, scholars, directors of art institutions, men of letters and government officials—in other words all those people who elsewhere would have been invaluable sources of information—he discovers that the Thai remain elusive not solely or even primarily as a consequence of historic or ethnic accidents but because they choose not to make themselves accessible to the foreigner. In their meetings with him, the Thai hold themselves politely, deliberately and determinedly aloof. Try though he may, all his efforts to learn about the people through contact with them come to nothing.

Not that this is immediately apparent. Although letters go unanswered and telephoning is ineffective, the Thai are not hard to meet so long as the visitor is prepared to make his calls at a venture. And when he does meet them, his reception is invariably polite, if not warm. This being so, the visitor is inclined to suppose the barrenness of the first meetings to be accidental. The senior monk, for example, who tells him the temple is "very old" and "quite important" is undoubtedly preoccupied by other less mundane matters, he thinks. The civil servant, reputedly an expert in cultural matters, who hides himself behind a defensive smile throughout the interview, might perhaps have been offended at some minor breach of etiquette. The man of letters, who spoke at such length and with such irrelevance, might simply have misunderstood his questions. So the visitor supposes, at least at first. But when he has met upwards of a dozen persons and gained nothing from them, he puts aside the theory of accidental misunderstandings and formulates other explanations for his failure.

For not only has he learned nothing from these people, he has had no mental contact with them. It is as if a glass wall surrounds the Thai. Invisible, impossible to delineate, more or less impenetrable, this wall shuts off the flow of sympathy without which there can be no true meeting of minds. Seeking to make the vital contact, the visitor encounters the smooth, blank, amorphous barrier; through it he can see the Thai with perfect clarity, observe his nods, smiles and gestures; and yet he is completely cut off from him. Time and again he seeks to establish the mental link, and time and again the wall rebuffs him. Eventually, convinced of the futility of trying to make contact, he gives up the attempt.

Even then, one major question is likely to continue to tantalize the visitor. Why should the Thai be so defensive? Is it because they know as little about their own culture as he does and wish to conceal their ignorance? Is it because the usages of Thai society prohibit the asking of probing questions? Does a suspicion of the foreigner, a legacy of the long struggle with the colonial powers, still linger? Is there a gulf between the two modes of thought too wide to be bridged? One question breeds a whole family of others, and each remains unanswered. Here, as elsewhere, the glass wall defeats him.

It is the object of this book to palliate the defeat. To do so, it presents two related Thai works of art, the bas-reliefs of Wat Phra Jetubon and the story they partially depict, the *Ramakien*. It would be presumptious to pretend that it furnishes a satisfactory introduction to the Thai, for there is no shortcut to intimacy with any people, even the most forthcoming, and there can be none with the Thai. The only route to a better understanding lies through a close study of the language, beliefs, customs, history and arts of the country and long firsthand acquaintance with the people. This proviso notwithstanding, this work seeks to introduce to the English speaker the most important theme in the neglected field of the Thai arts and, in so doing, to cast some light on the conceptual furnishings of the Thai mind. For, while a people may remain silent, their art at least may speak to us on their behalf.

Of the suitability of the *Ramakien* for such an undertaking, there can be no doubt. An offshoot of one of the world's great myth-sagas, the Indian *Ramayana*, it has been the dominant theme of Thai culture as far back as the culture can be traced. Its ramifications and great length preclude summary, but its kernel is the battle between the god-king Ram and the demon Totsagan for the possession of Ram's beautiful and virtuous wife, Nang Seeda. Gods, demons, angels, humans, animals and monsters participate in this conflict, and its venues include the forests and cities of proto-historic Thailand and the heavens and hells above and below them.

To appreciate the influence of this theme on the Thai culture, one has to envisage a work combining the popularity of the Arthurian legends, the literary force of the works of Shakespeare and the authority of the Bible, for the *Ramakien* has come to be the scepter of the Thai monarchy, the major source of artistic inspiration to the court, and the cosmogony, preceptor, and history of the people. Buddhism alone is a more pervasive religious influence, but even Buddhism takes second place to the *Ramakien* where the arts are concerned. Three major literary works and scores of minor ones are based on the theme, while the other media—painting, dance-drama and sculpture among them—are dominated by it to a similar degree. The young Thai first hears the story at home, learns it more thoroughly at school and university, and continues to meet it in later life in such varied forms as comic strips, films, and magazine condensations. The *Ramakien* thus maintains its preeminence both as a classic and as a popular story.

To the Westerner, to whom the magic in the works of Shakespeare and the miracles in the Bible are impediments not only to belief but also to appreciation, the influence and popularity of the *Ramakien* will doubtless be unaccountable. How can a work in which magic and the supernatural play so large a part, and which is therefore divorced from and at variance with the world at large, maintain its hold on the Thai, he will wonder. And it is here one encounters a major difference between the Thai view of the world and that of a Westerner.

So far as the Thai are concerned, extraordinary though it may seem to the outsider, there is nothing about the *Ramakien* that is at variance with the world around them. On the contrary, the *Ramakien* is an analogue of the Thai view of life and the world. The features of this epic world may be heightened and exaggerated, but its roots are no less firmly planted in reality, as far as the Thai are concerned, than those of the Western literary classics. To be specific, just as the trees, flowers and animals of the *Ramakien* accurately represent what can be seen in rural Thailand today, so too the supernatural beliefs and practices of the story faithfully reflect those of the modern Thai. The hero of the *Ramakien* is an incarnation of the god Narai—so too is the present ruler. The world of the *Ramakien* teems with demons and spirits, who must be fought or placated—so too does the twentieth-century Thai world. The events of the *Ramakien* are predicted and controlled by hermits and haruspex: in modern Thailand, cabinet ministers consult astrologers, the movements of the market are predicted by Buddhist monks, and miracles occur daily. No one who has lived in Thailand (or elsewhere in Southeast Asia for that matter) can have failed to observe that to the people of the region the supernatural is commonplace.

If the supernatural elements present no impediment either to enjoyment or belief, neither does the story's remoteness in time. The Thai sense of historical perspective is not well developed. In the absence of reliable records and chronicles, the past is a timeless continuum, in which fact and fiction, history and legend are indistinguishable from one another. In this continuum, it is not easy to say who is the more remote, who the more real, the fictitious Ram of Ayutaya or the historical Ram Kamheng of Sukhothai.

If this is the case—if, in other words, there is a close correspondence between the world glimpsed through the pages of the *Ramakien* and that seen through the eyes of the modern Thai—the wonder is not that there should be so little contact between the Thai and the Westerner, but that there should be as much as there is. For if the analogy holds, the world beheld by the Thai is a dim and mysterious forest in which the dark gods are still powerful. The Western view, it need hardly be added, is a little different. In the remote past there was a correspondence between the two, but since those times the Western forests have been felled, the sacred groves cleared and the land put to the plough.   The gods have been banished, and in their place the austere trinity of the scientific world—reason, order and coherence—reigns.   The gulf between the two views—the consequence of a thousand years of Western cultural, religious and industrial revolutions—is not lightly to be bridged.

To draw this parallel between the Thai world and that of the *Ramakien* is not to ignore the fact that the version of the story now current in Thailand was composed nearly two hundred years ago, at a time when Western influence in the country was minimal.   In the interim, the changes have been radical and far-reaching.   While the peasant continues to lead a life untouched by all but a few material products of the West, the small but powerful urban middle class, which seized control of the country from the monarchy in 1932, has been stimulated and is still sustained by Western ideas and methods.   Many members of this class—scholars, politicians and businessmen—are educated abroad and spend much of their working time in contact with foreigners.   Can it then be said that these people continue to live in the *Ramakien* world, despite the events of recent years?

The answer is that it can and they do.   There can be no question of the importance of the changes wrought by the country's contacts with the West, nor any doubt that these changes will quicken and intensify in the coming years.   But the Thai are a tenaciously conservative people, and material changes introduced from the outside world are not accompanied by corresponding changes in their mentality.   On the contrary, they are more often productive of a psychological reaction.   The reformers who have appeared from time to time in their history—both kings and commoners—have had some success in altering their way of life; they have had far less in changing their ways of thought.

The member of the middle class consequently lives in two disharmonious worlds: that of his traditions, and that introduced by the West.   On the one hand, he is eager for the material benefits that Western methods bring him.   On the other, he is averse to the changes in which they threaten to involve him.   Between the two worlds he leads an uneasy double life, commuting daily (so to speak) between his forest home with its spirit shrine and his air-conditioned office in town.   Perhaps his uneasiness is unnecessary, for other peoples in much the same situation—notably the Hindus—carry off the double life with aplomb, even to the extent of reproaching the West for its materialism while depending upon it for survival.   The Thai, however, has neither the cultural self-assurance of the Hindu nor his love of contention.   Faced with the contradictions of his present way of life, he prefers evasion to confrontation.   The glass wall is a natural outcome.

If the more important literary works of this varied, interesting but baffling people were available in translation, there is no doubt that much of what remains obscure in Thai motivation, thought and behavior would become much clearer.   Given the compactness of the literature, translations of the three works forming the core of the Thai classics—the *Ramakien*, *Phra Apaimanee* and the *Inao*—would shed a great deal of light on the traditional furnishings of the Thai mind.   So far, however, no such translations have been published.   Until they are, this brief illustrated version of the *Ramakien* must provide what illumination it can.

FROM RAMAYANA TO RAMAKIEN

THE BAS-RELIEFS

FROM RAMAYANA TO RAMAKIEN

A literary and historical background
to the Thai epic

To understand why a Hindu theme should have been chosen by a Thai king for the decoration of a Buddhist temple, one has to glance back over the major events in the history of the Thai people since they emerged from the southern hills of China some nine hundred years ago to occupy what is now their homeland.

Prior to their arrival, the Thai had lived to the south of the Chinese empire in the independent kingdom of Nan Chao, and cursory mention of this kingdom by the Chinese in records of the time indicates that they considered the court of their neighbors far inferior in quality to their own, but not altogether different in kind. Pressures from the north, however, impelled the Thai to move from Nan Chao towards the less crowded and more fertile lands of the south, and the kingdom finally expired during the Mongol invasions of China in the thirteenth century. Historians assume—and there is very little of this period about which they can speak with assurance—that by the time the Thai had arrived in what was to become their own land, and there made contact with the great civilization of the Mon and Khmer, they had lost almost all the cultural characteristics they had shared with the Chinese and become a people hardy but untutored, tribal in organization and animist by religion.

Of their hardiness at least there can be little doubt. The greatest influx of the Thai into north Thailand occurred in the middle of the thirteenth century, and while at first they were content to form minor principalities within the domain and under the suzerainty of the Mon and Khmer, only fifty years passed before they united, temporarily at least, under one king, and took possession of the greater part of the area now comprising the Thai state. Only a further one hundred years were to elapse before they were strong enough to cast off their last bonds of allegiance and defeat the Khmer decisively, sacking their capital of Angkor in 1431. From that day until this—brief incursions by the Burmese and even briefer ones by the colonial powers notwithstanding—the Thai have remained the undisputed possessors of the richest rice plain in Southeast Asia and, what is even more to the point for an understanding of the Wat Phra Jetubon bas-reliefs, the inheritors of the civilization of the Khmer.

This civilization had been initiated by the Mon and developed and sustained within the empire of the people closely related to them, the Khmer. Of the extraordinary genius of this people, and of their remarkable

29

achievements, one can say no more in passing than that the fragments of their capital, Angkor, still to be seen in Cambodia today, bear them mute yet glorious witness.   This civilization, nevertheless, owed an incalculable debt to India, for all its arts and institutions—architecture, engineering, religions, system of kingship, dramatic and decorative arts—were flowers from the main stem of the Indian subcontinent, and, without the germinating influence of the early Indian colonization of the area, could never have come into being.   One should stress that the shaping influence was Indian entirely and exclusively, for while there were contacts between the Khmer and the Chinese, at least in the later stages of the development of the Southeast Asian empire, their effect on Khmer culture was negligible.

One aspect of this civilization that the Thai acquired and made their own was its religious dichotemy.   The Khmer embraced concurrently two exclusive Indian religious systems, Hinduism and Buddhism.   Until towards the end of the empire, these systems were separate, the former appertaining to the court, the latter to the people.   The kings reinforced their absolute temporal power by claiming to be the mortal representative, and indeed the incarnation, of one of the Hindu deities, and a temple was built for each that became on his death his funerary monument and cult center.   The people, meanwhile, finding in Buddhism the creed most suited to their situation, nevertheless paid homage to their god-king as a matter of course.   These systems were adopted by the Thai and modified by them to the extent that what had been a dichotemy became a duality. That is, while the religion of the court continued to be Hinduism, the Thai king became an adherent of his people's faith, thus acting as a linchpin between the two systems.

The seriousness with which the Thai kings have regarded their putative divinity is not easy to evaluate.   At the present time the Hindu element of the religious duality is still strongly in evidence in the rituals of the Thai court and state.   A chapter of Brahmin priests, for example, still attends and to a certain extent regulates the court and officiates at royal state ceremonies; and while perhaps few of his subjects continue to honor him as a deity, the king is even now cloaked by the forms and titles if not the full majesty of divinity. It is in any case of more than passing interest that the ashes of deceased monarchs are placed within the altars of royal temples, though the precise significance of this custom has yet to be defined.   The ashes of the founder of the present dynasty, King Rama I, are kept within the Phra Ubosot of Wat Phra Jetubon.

These facts go a long way towards explaining the choice of a Hindu theme for the bas-reliefs of Wat Phra Jetubon, but to understand why the particular theme, namely the *Ramakien*, was selected, it is necessary to know something of the history behind it.

The *Ramakien* is a variant of the Indian classic, the *Ramayana*, which was written some two thousand years ago by the poet Valmiki and has since become part of the literature of each of the regions of Southeast Asia.   It is a work of great length and considerable profundity, and takes second place in the Indian literary repertoire only to the *Mahabarata*.   In summary, it tells of the divine origin and mortal existence of the hero king of Ayodhia, Rama. It falls into three sections, of which the first deals mainly with the court intrigue leading to Rama's renunciation of the throne and exile; the second with the abduction of his wife Sita, the defeat of the demons of Lanka island and Sita's recovery; and the third with Rama's repudiation of his wife and her assumption into the underworld.

Exegesis has disclosed a number of levels to the *Ramayana*, mythological, historical, social and moral among them. Historians have drawn a parallel between the epic's account of the campaign against Lanka and the actual conquest of Ceylon by the Aryans, and anthropologists have suggested that Hanuman's act of fealty to Rama symbolizes the overthrow and assimilation of the earlier animist beliefs of the Dravidians by the elemental and cosmic gods of the invaders. On the literary level, too, scholars have found the *Ramayana* a rewarding study, observing that the Indian epic and Homer's *Iliad* share so many similarities, among them the basic theme of the ravished bride, that it is highly probable that they spring from a common source. Some, furthermore, have found a notable resemblance between the steadfastness of the evil Ravana (Totsagan in the Thai version) and the nobility of Lucifer in *Paradise Lost*, while others have traced back to Hanuman the genealogies of a thousand comic servants of elevated masters—from Wu Cheng-tu's Monkey to Cervantes' Sancho Panza and beyond, and have seen in that character's journey to Lanka the first step along the picaresque road that has been followed by so many wanderers since.

But interesting though these theories are, they have little bearing on the *Ramakien* and less on the Wat Phra Jetubon reliefs, and it is the purpose behind the writing of the *Ramayana* that sheds most light on these matters.

The *Ramayana* was composed as an encomium to the king of the realm of which Valmiki was a subject—a work designed to augment and perpetuate the transitory glories of the monarch's origin, conquests and court by making them the subject of a work of literature. By the talismanic qualities inherent in a work of art, it was further to guarantee the king's claim to identity with Rama, and through him with the godhead. The *Ramayana*, in other words, was the "Great Seal" of the king's divinity. Small wonder that it proved so popular throughout Southeast Asia, for wherever the struggle for power was fiercest the *Ramayana* was most in demand, both as a testament to the awful divinity of kingship by monarchs with an insecure tenure of the throne, and as a ready-made genealogy by those usurpers who had none. And nowhere was the struggle more bitter or the demand more urgent—if contemporary Western sources are to be believed—than at the Thai court of Ayudhia.

It can be assumed that the *Ramayana*, or one of its many variants, reached Southeast Asia around the beginning of the Christian era and had enjoyed a long life among the Mon and Khmer when the Thai entered the region. The reliefs of Angkor Wat, indeed, provide adequate testimony to the fact. With a similar confidence it can be assumed that the work was current in the Thai court from the thirteenth century, as one of the most famous of the early kings was entitled Ram Kamheng—Ram the Valiant. Its later standing can be gauged from the fact that the name chosen for capital of the kingdom—Ayudhia—was that of the legendary hero's city (Ayodhia in the *Ramayana*).   Unfortunately, any early written versions of the *Ramakien* (the Thai for "The Story of Rama") were lost when Ayudhia was destroyed by the Burmese in 1767.   As it is, the earliest known written rendering (*ca.* 1775) is that of King Taksin of Thonburi, while the version now accepted as the classic in Thailand is that of his successor, the founder of the dynasty now ruling, King Rama Jakri I.

It is not easy to estimate the extent to which Rama I drew on vernacular versions of the story handed down through the courts of the Mon and Khmer to Ayudhia and Bangkok, and to what extent he was obliged to return to contemporary Indian sources.   In the essentials—the ending excepted—his *Ramakien* closely follows the main lines of Valmiki's original, but the differences in detail are considerable and these differences—of incidents added or omitted, of names, customs, dress, character, location, flora, etc., changed—have imparted to the work an atmosphere and feeling that owes nothing to its source and everything to its Thai regenesis.   There is no place here for a detailed analysis of these changes, rewarding though such a study would be.   It can only be noted that their principal effect is to blur and soften, so that inexorabilities of development are avoided and moral exigencies relaxed—much as might be expected in the change from the Hindu milieu to the more easy-going Thai ambience.   In the *Ramakien*, for example, the main events of the original are reduplicated as far as the denouement, but whereas the *Ramayana* ends tragically with Sita parting from her husband, the *Ramakien* closes with a reconciliation arbitrated by the gods.   In characterization, furthermore, while Ram is recognizably Rama, as Lak is Lakshaman, Seeda is Sita and Ongkot is Angada (Totsagan and Ravana differ in name, but in character and motivation remain indistinguishable), the Thai Hanuman plays an altogether fuller and more important role than his Indian counterpart.   Not for him the chastity of the Hindu Hanuman; his amorous adventures provide one of the recurrent themes of the Thai narrative, while his tricks and exploits dominate the central episode to the extent that he replaces Phra Ram there as the most prominent character.   But the greatest change between the two works is wrought below the primary and secondary levels of plot and characterization, for in the incorporation of incidents extraneous to the Indian epic the Thai imagination has worked freely, and it is the narration of episodes like the night at Bohkoranee, the meeting with hermit Nart, the attempts to kill Hanuman, Benyagai's transmogrification and the building of the causeway that most sharply distinguishes the *Ramakien* from the *Ramayana* and lends it its particular Thai atmosphere.   For so successfully indeed has Rama I transmuted the epic with these additions that the majority of the Thai know nothing of its Indian origin, looking upon the *Ramakien* less as a work of art than a history of their royal house. And there can be no greater tribute to his genius, nor better evidence that the work fulfills the purpose for which he intended it, than that this should be the case.

It is in the light of this long history of the movements, conquests and annexations of the Thai people that the bas-reliefs of Wat Phra Jetubon should be considered.   The Thai were and continue to be animists, but their cultural acquisitions include the popular religion of Buddhism, which has little to do with either gods or kings, and one of the elitist cults of Hinduism, which raises the monarch to the status of a divinity. The people from whom these cultural systems were taken were defeated by the Thai, perhaps on account of the failure of either of their religions to perform what must be one of their most important functions—to bind the people in a common belief. For while the funerary temples of Angkor remain one of the wonders of the world, they also stand as a warning of the danger that threatens a society in which one social element is exalted disproportionately above all others. The excessive toll of the building of these temples led to the neglect and breakdown of the elaborate agricultural system, and that breakdown to the impoverishment and debilitation of the people. This at least is one explanation of the spectacular collapse of the Khmer kingdom in the fifteenth century. And this element of excess the Thai have been successful in avoiding, for rejecting consistency in favor of common sense, their monarch has retained his elitist personal cult, but at the same time linked himself with his people by adopting their own religion.

And the Phra Ubosot is perhaps a fitting monument to such common sense: a modest chapel decorated with an easily overlooked work of art, containing the relics of the king who wrote himself into a relationship with the gods. The priests tend it, and the people bring their flowers.

THE BAS-RELIEFS

The origin of the bas-reliefs
of Wat Phra Jetubon

The rubbings illustrating this volume are taken from the marble bas-reliefs of one of Bangkok's oldest temples, Wat Phra Jetubon. This temple predates the founding of the capital by a number of years but was extensively restored in 1825 at the order of the third monarch of the dynasty now reigning, King Rama Jakri III. The bas-reliefs, comprising 152 panels measuring approximately 45 centimeters square, are set in the outer wall of the gallery of the chapel known as the Phra Ubosot. They depict a related series of episodes from the *Ramakien*, and the skill with which they have been executed has produced a unique, if minor work of art.

Something of a mystery surrounds the origin of these reliefs. It has been generally accepted that they were made to the order of King Rama III during the restoration of Wat Phra Jetubon, but there are now reasons to suppose they were executed in the old capital, Ayudhia, at an earlier date, and only brought to Bangkok later, perhaps in Rama III's reign.

The most cogent argument in favor of the Bangkok origin of the reliefs is the somewhat negative one that they are now at Wat Phra Jetubon, and there is no definite evidence of them having been elsewhere. But this same lack of evidence is also one of the weaknesses of the supposition that the reliefs were made for their present site. For when the temple was restored, a great deal of work was done: buildings were reconstructed and strengthened, images and statuary were acquired from other parts of the country, tablets with inscriptions about the arts and sciences of the time were set up, and artists and craftsmen were commissioned to redecorate the buildings. Records existing at the present give details of all this work. But concerning the *Ramakien* reliefs, nothing—or almost nothing—is to be found. The earliest comment on them appears to be that contained in a letter written by Prince Narit to his brother Prince Damrong (*Collected Letters*; 24 August, 1935) in which Prince Narit mentions the reliefs in passing and offers the opinion that they might be the work of a craftsman famous in Rama III's time, one Nai Jai, later Luang Prom Pichit, adding by way of explanation that Jai had supervised the restoration of the part of the temple in which the Phra Ubosot stands. Other references to the reliefs postdate Prince Narit's letter and offer nothing new on the subject of their origin.

Lack of information alone, however, might not have cast doubt on the assumption that the reliefs were made in Bangkok for Wat Phra Jetubon.   But there is another (and to Western, eyes at least, major) impediment to the acceptance of this assumption.   The panel series appears to be incomplete.

It should be explained here that the *Ramakien* falls into three sections, of which the second and most popular, the abduction and recovery of Nang Seeda, is the theme of the reliefs.   The first panels of the Wat Phra Jetubon series depict the abduction of Seeda, and the others, with great clarity and artistry, show the steps leading to the investment of Longka and the series of battles culminating in the death of Intorachit.   But while the written *Ramakien* then continues to mount to the great climax, the defeat of Totsagan and the recovery of Seeda, the reliefs conclude with the death of a character dismissed in the narrative version as of minor importance.*   Following this magnificently depicted story round the walls of the Phra Ubosot, and being brought to this unsatisfactory conclusion, one cannot escape the conviction that whoever planned the work saw it as a whole and intended it to end at the climactic moment of the defeat of Longka and the recovery of the goddess.   If this conviction is valid, the question arises why this intention should have been frustrated.

It needs to be stressed that this conviction, and the question it prompts, is the product of a Western viewpoint. Of the numerous Thai scholars and men of letters consulted in this matter, only one conceded that the ending of the reliefs as they now stand might be considered unsatisfactory.   All made the identical observation that while the artist might have wished to end the panels with the death of Totsagan and the recovery of Seeda, he had obviously found that there was not enough space around the building to do so.   Some added that there was in any case no need to conclude the story, as all Thais knew it by heart and could visualize for themselves what was not shown.   One observed that the continuity of a narrative was not to be expected in a pictorial work intended simply as decoration.   The only person who agreed that the ending might be considered unsatisfactory, added by way of qualification, "Of course, as an artist I feel the panels must end with the recovery of Seeda, but as a Thai..." and with a laugh and vague gesture, he left the rest unspoken.

One should add at this point that strong internal support for the supposition that the reliefs were made for their present situation and no other is provided by the grouping of the panels around the Phra Ubosot.   The line of the story runs from right to left around the chapel, and in the main each panel carries the events a step forward.   However, in many cases pairs of panels—and in one case three—compose a single scene and are

---

* It is interesting that this character, Sahatsadecha, should be indistinguishable from Totsagan, wearing as he does a headdress with many faces.   The unofficial guides to the temple point to the final panels and inform the visitor that Totsagan is there being given his quietus by Hanuman—the demon's concubine, of course, becoming Nang Seeda. And perhaps, there is a clue here to the incompleteness of the series.   It is not inconceivable that somewhere between the salvaging of the panels from the ruins of Ayudhia (if in fact they did originate there) and their final selection and arrangement at Wat Phra Jetubon, a similar error was made that was not corrected while it was possible, and now— for lack of the other panels—never can be.

meant to be viewed together. Furthermore, episodes within the story range from two to sixteen panels in length. The structure of the gallery itself imposes its own groupings on the panels, abutments dividing them into groups of three, six, seven, seven, six and three on the two shorter ends of the building and into eleven groups of four on each of the longer sides. This being the case, one might have expected that if the bas-reliefs had been planned for another building, the natural groupings according to the story and the groups into which the structure of Wat Phra Jetubon has forced them would have shown some disharmony, abutments separating panels meant to be viewed together and causing unnatural breaks in the episodes. In fact there is no single instance of paired panels being cut from their companions, and the episodes, despite the fact that the longer of them have to bridge abutments, show a distinct conformity with the divisions of the gallery walls. If the reliefs were brought to Bangkok from a building in Ayudhia, this conformity could only have been achieved by discarding panels that were not essential to the story.

The case for the reliefs having been made specifically for Wat Phra Jetubon may be summed up as follows: they are there now, and there is no record of them having been brought in from elsewhere; the division of the panels conforms with the structure of the chapel; and the ending is regarded, from a Thai viewpoint, as having no relevance to the issue of origin.

The case for believing the reliefs to have been planned for another building rests mainly on the conviction that no artist of the caliber of the creator of this series could have allowed it to end as it does at Wat Phra Jetubon through either indifference or lack of foresight. The supposition follows that the work is incomplete, and that not less than ten and possibly a great many more panels are missing. In this context it is of interest that at the present, the number of verses inscribed on separate tablets below the panels, which more or less refer to the action depicted in them, is the same as the number of panels now to be seen at the temple, 152, while a work entitled *The Collected Inscriptions of Wat Phra Jetubon*, compiled some forty years ago, gives the number of verses as 154. No trace is now to be found of the two missing tablets.

That the reliefs originated in Ayudhia rests on stronger evidence. No work of comparable quality or similar style is to be found in Bangkok. In Ayudhia, on the other hand, the capital of the kingdom until its sack and destruction by the Burmese in the eighteenth century and the source afterwards of many works of art now in Bangkok, three panels depicting scenes from the *Ramakien*, identical in style, stone and size to those of Wat Phra Jetubon, have been found and are now housed in the two museums there. A European resident of Thailand told the author that between the world wars it had been possible to find many other panels in Ayudhia, but that they were taken up by dealers and sold abroad.

There is little more to add to the matter, other than that the most fruitful field for further enquiry appears to lie in the direction of comparative analysis of the style of this and other works. Until this is done, or unless information of a more conclusive cast comes to light, the question of the origin of the reliefs will remain open.

THE RAMAKIEN

Prologue

THE DESTRUCTION OF THE DEMONS

Epilogue

NOTE: *Although the actual order of the bas-reliefs in Wat Phra Jetubon is from right to left, as shown in the "List of Bas-relief Panels," they are presented here in numerical order. However, where more than one panel depicts a single action, the original order has been preserved, so that, for example, panel 7 appears on the page before panel 6.*

PROLOGUE

Long ago in the court of the heavenly King Phra Isuan,* a thoughtless joke played by a group of celestial courtiers on one of their number led—as these things often do—to a quarrel. So bitter did this quarrel become that even the death of a number of those involved failed to bring the factions to their senses, and it was agreed that the matter should be settled by a combat on earth between the courtier who considered himself injured by the joke, an embittered, ill-favored creature named Nontok, and the favorite of King Isuan, handsome Phra Narai, who had erred only in good-naturedly accepting the role of mediator in the dispute. As a result of this agreement, Phra Narai consented to be born as Phra Ram, the son of the king of Ayutaya city, while his enemy Nontok became Totsagan, demon prince of the island state of Longka.

This demon prince, who was endowed with ten heads, twenty arms and a formidable battery of occult accomplishments, was born with a disposition as evil as any to be found in the Three Realms of Heaven, Earth and the Underworld, and the passage of the years developed and refined this disposition rather than diminished it. On the death of his father, Totsagan succeeded to the throne of Longka, from which he could muster a huge army of giants and demons and at the same time be sure of the loyal support of spirits, fiends and elementals as far throughout the earth and underworld as his infamy was current. His three brothers oddly enough, for all that they were demons, were comparatively well intentioned, and his principal wife Nang Monto enjoyed an excellent reputation—as female demons go—as a faithful wife and a loving mother. Their child Intorachit, on the other hand, was in all respects his father's son.

Somewhere on the mainland, deep in the forest, lay the monkey metropolis of Keetkin. This city was created when the divine Isuan, foreseeing that the conflict between Phra Ram and Totsagan was soon to take place and that his favorite would need an army to pit against that of the demon king, ordered his liegeman Phra In and the Sun God Phra Artit to attend to the matter. In compliance with his order the two gods came to earth and made love to a hermit's wife. Two fine boys, with visages of green and gold like their fathers', were born to the

---

* The titles "Phra" and "Nang" are the equivalents of "Lord" and "Lady" respectively and invariably precede personal names (Isuan, Ram, Seeda, Monto, etc.) of the gods and their avatars.

woman and were named Palee and Sukreep. One day, however, the daughter of the hermit maliciously disclosed to her father the true parentage of his wards, at which the angry man cursed his wife and sons, turning the former into a stone and the latter into a pair of monkeys. In her turn the mother cursed the daughter, condemning her to stand on the slopes of Mount Jakrawan, with one leg propped up on the bough of a tree, until the Wind God fathered a monkey son on her. The offspring of this singular union, named Hanuman, turned out to be a monkey of extraordinary magical gifts, and after various adventures he joined his uncles in the city of Keetkin, which by this time had been built for them by their fathers.

For a while the three monkeys lived in amity, Palee ruling the city as king with Sukreep acting as his regent. They treated their innumerable monkey subjects with justice and maintained friendly relations with neighboring forest states. A dispute between Palee and Sukreep over the ownership of a woman, however, led to the flight of Sukreep and his exile in the forest, where at the beginning of this story he patiently awaits the coming of Phra Narai, who is to redress the injustice of which he has been the victim.

Across the strait from Longka and scores of leagues across the mainland at the other side of the great forest, the young Phra Ram grew up as heir to the throne of Ayutaya, his virtues testifying as clearly to his divine origin as his becoming complexion of green. Only slightly less excellent than himself were his three brothers Lak, Phrot and Satroot, and the sight of the four boys as they played in the flower garden of the palace, or learned to use the bow and the sword, or studied the arts of kingship and the secrets of the universe under their hermit tutors daily gladdened the heart of Ayutaya's king. When in due course he came to manhood, Phra Ram was married to the lovely Nang Seeda, the daughter of the ruler of the neighboring city of Mitila, in a ceremony honored by the gods and celebrated by all men.

Now this young lady had a curious history. As Lakshmi, the celestial consort of Phra Narai, she had permitted herself to be born on earth in order to share the mortal adventures of her lord and chose as her parents Nang Monto and Totsagan. At the moment of her birth in Longka she had uttered a cry defying the demons, and as it was predicted that she would be the cause of the death of Totsagan and the downfall of Longka, she had been cast adrift on the sea in a glass bowl. The gods and angels having protected the abandoned child, she had been found, nurtured, and educated as his own daughter by the childless king of Mitila. It is hardly necessary to add that Nang Seeda's grace, beauty, and virtue surpassed by far those qualities in any other woman.

The marriage of the royal couple, less the joining of man and wife in wedlock than the union of sun and moon, cast an added luster over the city of Ayutaya, and it seemed at first that the Golden Age had been restored to the world. This almost universal happiness, however, was of short duration. The king was advanced in years by this time and announced his intention of relinquishing the throne in favor of Phra Ram. One of his wives, acting at the instigation of a hunchbacked and malevolent servant, demanded that he repay a debt of honor to her by placing her own son Phrot on the throne for fourteen years, banishing Phra Ram to the forest during this period.   To his intense grief, the king was obliged to accede to her demands.   Ram accepted the situation with equanimity.   He tried to persuade Nang Seeda to remain in the palace, but when she insisted that it was a wife's duty and privilege to share whatever hardships were her husband's lot, Phra Ram yielded to her pleas and permitted her to accompany him.   With the blessing of the dying king, the royal couple left the palace and, accompanied by Phra Lak, entered the forest.

THE DESTRUCTION OF THE DEMONS

THE ABDUCTION OF NANG SEEDA

Imagine a forest, deep, dim and mysterious, stretching away on all sides.   Above it shines a hot sun, but only the occasional ray pierces the thick roof of leaves and strikes down to the mossy ground, and the air is still, moist and cool.   Beyond a curtain of creepers a stream runs over a rock ledge into a small pool.   Here butterflies and scintillating dragonflies flaunt their colors over the dun water, as brilliant as the flowers of the bank and far more subtle.   Beneath the surface of the pool, fish as old and grey as stones hover on tremulous fins.

The only constant sound is the murmur of the stream.   Now and again, somewhere in the distance, a bird— like no bird you have ever seen—ripples forth its call, or the cicadas strike up their mindless music, or a beast crashes unseen among the upper branches.

There is no change here, no calendar, no time; only a succession of muted days and starless nights.

Here, far from Ayutaya, Phra Ram, Nang Seeda and Phra Lak have made their home.

---

1. *Phra Ram returns with the magic deer and meets Phra Lak*

One day, in distant Longka, Totsagan, the King of the Demons, hears of the beauty of Nang Seeda and determines that she shall become one of his wives.   Nang Monto, his own favorite, warns him that Ram is the incarnation of the god Narai and that the abduction of Seeda can only be followed by war.   Totsagan, however, has already made up his mind and is not to be deterred.

Early in the morning, accompanied by Mareet, one of his subjects, he mounts his chariot and flies over the ocean and forest until he comes to the Kotawaree River, near which the royal hermits have their hut.

At Totsagan's instruction, Mareet changes himself into a gazelle.   He darts across the clearing before the eyes of Nang Seeda and disappears into the undergrowth.   Enchanted by the beauty of the animal, Seeda implores her lord either to catch it or bring her its magnificent pelt.   Phra Ram suspects that the beast is a piece of enchantment but overcoming his foreboding takes his bow and follows the gazelle into the forest, having first warned his brother to guard Nang Seeda well.

Mareet, with terror in his heart, flies deeper and deeper into the forest, but Ram at last corners the beast and

1. *Phra Ram returns with the magic deer and meets Phra Lak*

mortally wounds it. Mareet falls, as he does so crying out in Phra Ram's voice, "Oh, Lak, help me. I am trapped by a demon. Help, help!"

The call rings through the forest to the hermit's hut, but Lak, knowing that no mere demon could bring about his brother's end, remains with Nang Seeda. She, however, now distracted at the thought that Phra Ram is in danger, entreats Lak to go to his aid and, when he still hesitates, taunts him for his cowardice and worse, accuses him of hoping that if his brother dies, she, Nang Seeda, will become his wife. Seeing that it is useless to reason with the distraught Seeda, Phra Lak prostrates himself dutifully before her and hurries off into the forest, hoping to return within a matter of minutes.

Seeda is left alone.

2. Totsagan abducts Nang Seeda

This is the moment that the demon king has been waiting for. Having transformed himself into an old anchorite, he hobbles before Nang Seeda, greets the lovely lady in a quavering voice, and asks her name. His eyes meanwhile feed on the perfection of face and form before him, the like of which he has seen nowhere in all the Three Worlds, at once inflaming his desire and strengthening his determination to make her his own. Her voice too, as she tells him she is Seeda, the wife of Phra Ram, seems that of an angel rather than a mere mortal.

Craftily he asks her, "How is it that you—with the attributes of a goddess—live here in the wilderness? Why, at the expression of the desire, you could be the bride of Totsagan, the King of Longka."

At these words Nang Seeda feels a deadly coldness invade her limbs, but she replies indignantly, "In the eyes of gods and men alike, the demon Tostagan is a criminal, and Phra Narai, in his incarnation as Phra Ram, is foredestined to crush him."

Even as the last word leaves her lips the anchorite vanishes, and in his place stands Totsagan, the ten-headed, the twenty-armed. Wasting no more time, he seizes Nang Seeda and, despite her struggles and despairing cries for help, firmly grasping her slender limbs in his many hands, he lifts her into his waiting chariot and soars up high above the forest. Held fast, weeping, overcome with fear and shame, Seeda calls on her husband for help, but her cries fall on the empty air.

3. The bird Sadayu attacks Totsagan

But the air is not entirely empty. Gliding in and out of the small clouds, soaring in the sunlight above the forest is the heavenly Sadayu. This great bird has long been a friend of the king of Ayutaya and of his children, and seeing that Seeda is in trouble he immediately stoops to the attack, crying as he falls, "You ten-headed blackguard, prepare to meet your doom!"

Totsagan, furious at being insulted by a mere bird, prepares to dispatch his assailant. When Sadayu clashes

with the enemy, however, striking left and right with powerful wings and needle-sharp talons, the demons of Totsagan's bodyguard rain lifeless from the air. The two thousand lions drawing the demon's chariot are similarly destroyed, and Totsagan and his prize are thrown roughly to the earth. His weapons scattered, his demons destroyed, the King of Longka draws what seems likely to be his last breath when the great bird sings out in triumph:

> "Your death is here, O criminal king,
> For you are mortal, whereas I
> Am told that I need never die
> Unless I'm struck by Isuan's ring."

Hearing this, Totsagan immediately tears Phra Isuan's ring from Seeda's finger and hurls it at the bird. Transformed into a hissing discus, the ring breaks the bird's mighty wings and lodges in his breast. With the wind sighing through his broken feathers, Sadayu crashes to earth. There he plucks the ring from his breast and, mortally wounded, awaits the coming of Phra Ram.

Totsagan reanimates his creatures, mounts his chariot once more, and flies on with captive Seeda to Longka.

---

4. *Hanuman and Sukreep pay homage to Phra Ram with Phra Lak in attendance*

For some time the grief-stricken royal brothers wander through the forest, from Sadayu learning the identity of Seeda's abductor and from giants whom they defeat that they can hope to gain allies for their campaign against Longka from the monkey kingdoms of Keetkin and Chompoo.

Eventually they come to the grove where Hanuman, the magic monkey, is meditating. The Wind God Phra Pai stirs up a breeze in which he has skillfully combined the scents of many flowers, and the two heroes, overtaken by an irresistible lassitude, lie down under a large and shady tree and sleep. Hanuman, having broken off his meditation to collect some fruit, comes on them and, curious to know who they can be, throws down pieces of twig onto the sleepers.

Phra Lak awakes and, seeing the little white monkey on the branch above, reaches up a hand to catch it. Hanuman skips onto a higher branch, however, and dances this way and that as Lak tries to dislodge him with the end of his bow. Phra Ram awakes and immediately recognizes the monkey with its diamond pelt, brilliant earrings, and jeweled teeth as the talented Hanuman. The Son of the Wind for his part looks down at Phra Ram and sees that he has been recognized, thinking to himself, "This fine prince knows who I am, so it must be the god I've been instructed to serve, Phra Narai." Delighted to have met his future master, Hanuman swings down out of the tree and prostrates himself before Phra Ram, while the favorite of Isuan, no less pleased to have at last encountered the able monkey, strokes Hanuman's back. When the formalities have been

3. *The bird Sadayu attacks Totsagan*

46

4. *Hanuman and Sukreep pay homage to Phra Ram with Phra Lak in attendance*

48

5. *Sukreep challenges Palee*

49

observed, Hanuman fetches and introduces his uncle Sukreep to Phra Ram, explaining that it has been ordained that as Phra Narai he shall end the life of the unrighteous king of Keetkin, Palee, and elevate Sukreep to the vacant throne.

Phra Ram agrees to help Sukreep, and it is arranged that in the course of a fight between the two brothers, Phra Ram—as the divine Narai—shall shoot Palee from ambush with the arrow Promat.

5. *Sukreep challenges Palee*

Sukreep flies to Palee's palace in Keetkin and loudly and with many insults challenges his brother to single combat. Palee, with burning ears, seizes his sword and flies at Sukreep. Near at hand, in the guise of a hermit, Phra Narai waits for a chance to end the combat, but the brothers are so similar in appearance that he cannot distinguish between them. The outcome is that Palee gains the upper hand and, unwilling to kill Sukreep on account of the affection he still feels for him, disarms his brother and throws him down to earth in the vicinity of Mount Jakrawan.

Little the worse for wear, but extremely put out, Sukreep makes his way back to Phra Narai and asks him why he failed to keep his promise. The god explains his difficulty and, having bound an armlet to Sukreep's wrist so as to be able to distinguish between him and his brother, tells him to return to the palace and challenge Palee once more.

6. *Phra Narai fires at Palee*
7. *Palee, fighting with Sukreep, catches Phra Narai's arrow*

This time Palee determines to end the matter once and for all. Grasping his sword, he flies out of the palace window and straight for his brother. The swords flash in the air, and the combatants rain blow after blow on each other, Sukreep pretending to give ground but in fact leading Palee to the place where Phra Narai lies in ambush. When he sees his opportunity, the god bends his bow and lets loose the Promat arrow, but Palee sees the shaft coming and plucks it out of the air. Turning to Phra Narai, he shouts angrily: "Hermit, what has this quarrel to do with you that you should try to kill me?"

Phra Narai holds his bow aloft in his four hands and says, "I am Phra Ram Jakri, and I have come to earth to vanquish the demons. Think of the wrongs you have done, Palee, and accept your punishment."

When Palee hears this, he knows his end has come. He takes his leave of Sukreep and charges him to serve Phra Ram faithfully. "As king," he says, "you must do no wrong. Banish hatred and be governed by good intentions. To your people be as a father, and to your enemies a scourge."

Then Palee stabs himself with Narai's arrow, and his soul leaves his body to be received into paradise.

When the news of his death reaches Keetkin, the court and the people are united in mourning for their king.

A procession leaves the palace, headed by Dara, Palee's wife, Ongkot who is his son by Nang Monto, and Chompooparn, Hanuman's childhood companion. They make their obeisances to Sukreep, who is now their lord, and pay homage to Phra Narai, who rejoices when he sees what fine soldiers these little monkey people will make.

The funeral ceremonies are quickly arranged. With one arrow shot from his bow, Narai creates a diamond cremation sala and a crystal urn to hold Palee's remains; with a second, he lights the funeral pyre. Sukreep, Dara and the sons of the king throw flowers and ornaments of gold into the fire, and soon the flames have consumed Palee's corpse.

Sukreep, the new king of Keetkin, is borne back to the city by the people.

7. *Palee, fighting with Sukreep, catches Phra Narai's arrow*

52

6. *Phra Narai fires at Palee*

9. *Sukreep and Ongkot and other generals receive their orders*

8. *Phra Ram, with Phra Lak and Hanuman, orders the Longka reconnaissance*

8. *Phra Ram, with Phra Lak and Hanuman, orders the Longka reconnaissance*

9. *Sukreep and Ongkot and other generals receive their orders*

Sukreep busies himself in Keetkin with the mustering of an army for Phra Ram and, because the city has never known war, finds difficulty in raising enough monkeys of the right age and experience to serve as quartermasters, armorers, and sergeants at arms, let alone staff officers and generals. Consequently he sends to his neighbor and ally, the great Chompoo, who willingly agrees to serve with Phra Ram and undertakes to help make up the deficiencies in Sukreep's muster.

While all this preparation is going on, Phra Ram orders a reconnaissance party to make itself ready to penetrate Longka's walls to discover what has happened to Nang Seeda and, if possible, to let her know that her rescue is being prepared. Sukreep, as commander in chief of the army, appoints Hanuman, Chompooparn and Ongkot to lead this party on its hazardous mission.

Hanuman is entrusted with two tokens by which Seeda shall know that they truly come from Phra Ram, the first Phra Isuan's ring, taken from the dying Sadayu, the other her breast cloth, which she dropped on the way to Longka. Hanuman accepts them but offers the opinion that they might just as well have been found by the demons and respectfully asks Phra Ram if there is any more intimate token that will put at rest the doubts Nang Seeda might have about their authenticity.

So Phra Ram surrenders the most personal memory that he shares with Nang Seeda.

"Remind her of the first glance we two exchanged in Mitila town, when our eyes met and we saw love bloom like forest flowers after rain. Tell her of this, and she will know you come from me," he says.

And with that, the reconnaissance party sets forth.

10. *Hanuman leads the monkeys towards Longka*

For some days the reconnaissance party pushes on through the echoing forest towards Longka. One evening the monkeys come to the Bohkoranee Pond, on whose banks flowers grow in such profusion that no one who lingers nearby can escape falling into an enchanted sleep.

11. *Baklan sees the sleeping monkeys*

Beneath the lotus-starred surface of the pond lurks Baklan, a creature banished from heaven for his drunken lewdness during a celestial banquet and condemned to serve a term as the demon watchman of the pond. Seeing

10. *Hanuman leads the monkeys towards Longka*

11. *Baklan sees the sleeping monkeys*

only the loveliness of the place and knowing nothing of its dangers, the monkeys choose to spend the night there. After a frugal meal of fruit and the practice of martial exercises under the direction of the zealous Hanuman, the monkeys dispose themselves about the bank and drop into a profound slumber.

12. *Baklan fights with Ongkot*

At midnight, Baklan comes to the surface of the pond and sees the sleeping monkeys. With murder in his heart, he creeps onto the bank and seizes Ongkot. As the monster attempts to crush him, Ongkot gradually wakens from his heavy sleep and realizes with some difficulty that he is being attacked. Throwing off his deadly languor, the son of Palee grapples with the monster, beats him to his knees, and seizes his sword. Strong as he is, Baklan is no match for Ongkot and is quickly reduced to suing for mercy, whimpering in astonishment, "Such a little monkey, and yet so strong."

"Little monkey indeed," shouts Ongkot angrily. "I'll have you know you're dealing with no less than a soldier of Phra Narai, you watery oaf."

13. *Ongkot sends Baklan to heaven*

Baklan is overjoyed to hear these words, for when sentencing him for his misconduct, the celestial judge had said that his banishment should end when he was beaten in a conflict with a warrior of Phra Narai. He hastens to explain this to Ongkot, throwing himself at his feet. Palee's son recognizes the ring of truth about the story and performs the appropriate ceremony for returning the earthbound Baklan to heaven—that is, he strokes the monster's back from nape to tail and up he rises into the dark night air.

14. *Hanuman makes love to Butsa Malee*

During their long journey to Longka, the monkeys one day come on a city in the jungle. A moat surrounds it, and its thick stone walls are surmounted by sturdy turrets. Beyond the walls, the roofs of a fine palace can be seen, and yet the gate is unguarded and the streets appear to be empty. Reconnoitering this deserted and eery city with caution, Hanuman and Ongkot are astonished to encounter a lovely creature, a woman of more than earthly beauty, in front of one of the palace gates. With great respect, Hanuman puts some questions to her and learns that the city is called Mayan. She gives her name as Butsa Malee and explains with some embarrassment that she has been its sole inhabitant since Phra Isuan banished her thirty thousand years ago for certain indiscretions. Having said so much, the divine creature suddenly slips past them into the palace grounds, bolting the door in their faces.

Not in the least deterred by this, Hanuman tells Ongkot to wait for him, vaults over the palace wall, and pursues the lady into the palace.

13. *Ongkot sends Baklan to heaven*

60

14. *Hanuman makes love to Butsa Malee*

Hanuman catches up with his graceful quarry in a large and spendid audience chamber. "Not so fast, my pretty," he says familiarly, "there are things I want to talk to you about."

Annoyed and perhaps a little alarmed at the monkey's persistence, Butsa Malee adopts a haughty tone. "It is true that I have been away from the heavenly court for some time now," she says, "but even so I doubt if it has become the custom for maidens of good breeding to consort with common monkeys. Kindly leave this palace immediately and go back to the forest where you belong."

"Common monkey!" says Hanuman indignantly. "You are speaking to Hanuman, the darling of the gods, the scourge of the demons."

Butsa Malee laughs at this. "Hanuman, you puny imposter, has four heads and eight arms. Phra Isuan told me that he can fly in the air and exhale stars with every breath. And by virtue of his powers, he is supposed to end my term of banishment and send me back to heaven. No more of your lies. Off with you, before you receive the punishment you deserve."

Immediately he hears this, Hanuman transforms himself into his celestial double and, leaping into the air, breathes suns, moons and stars into the audience chamber.

Overcome by astonishment and terror, Butsa Malee flees into her inner chamber, with Hanuman, who has reverted to his terrestrial form, pursuing her. There, using all his wiles, the personable monkey closes with the flustered maiden, charms away her fears with sweet words and soft caresses, and in a very short time enjoys her love.

15. *Hanuman returns Butsa Malee to heaven*

After this delightful interlude, Hanuman—never one to lose his wits in such a situation—asks Butsa Malee how best to get to Longka. She tells him, adding, "On the way you will come to a stream, where my sister, the angel Suwanna Malee, lives. When you meet her, promise me you will do one thing."

"Anything, my love," says Hanuman.

"She too has been banished from heaven, to live on earth for a term. When you meet her, treat her as you have treated me and release her from her mortal bondage."

Hanuman, not in the least averse to such an undertaking, assures her that he will do so. He leads Butsa Malee from the palace and, after performing the appropriate ceremonies, casts her up into the air. Transformed into a radiant young goddess, Butsa Malee soars upwards, and is readmitted to the heavenly court.

16. *The monkeys meet the bird Sampatee*

After many more adventures, Hanuman and his companions reach the snow capped mountains of Hematiwan, which stand on the coast of the mainland opposite the island of Longka. They climb the mountain and

15. *Hanuman returns Butsa Malee to heaven*

16. *The monkeys meet the bird Sampatee*

near the summit come on the great bird Sampatee crouched featherless and shivering within a cave. Hanuman greets the bird and tells him of the noble death of his brother Sadayu.

Sampatee weeps to hear this story. Then, in his turn, tells the monkeys why he is in the cave, and how he lost his feathers.

"Long ago," he says, "when I was much younger and my brother was little more than a fledgling, our mother left us for a time, having warned me to watch carefully over Sadayu and see he came to no harm. For a time, all was well, but then Sadayu grew restless and, while my attention was elsewhere, flew out of the nest and high above the forest trees. There, for the first time, he caught sight of the orb of the sun spinning through the heavens and, taking it to be a golden fruit, flew high into the sky, meaning to pluck and eat it. Just in time to save him from the anger of Phra Artit, the Sun God, I saw what had happened and flew above him, guiding him back to safety while protecting him from the god's hot darts. He reached the nest unharmed, but Phra Artit's curse seared every feather from my body, and I was condemned to live in this cave until Phra Ram's army passes."

To the bird's joy, Hanuman informs him that they are a reconnaissance party from Phra Ram's army. With Sampatee's permission the three generals seat themselves on his back, and at once the bird's splendid plumage is restored. He stretches out his powerful wings, launches himself into the wind, and with the three monkeys riding on his back swirls up high into the sky. From there he indicates, far across the ocean, the bulk of the blue hills of Longka, their destination.

They return to the Hematiwan Mountains. Hanuman instructs his brother generals to wait for him there. Sampatee flies back to Phra Ram's army to bring him the news of their progress, while the Son of the Wind soars up into the air and, after a backward glance at the mainland, flies out over the ocean in the direction of Longka.

17. *Hanuman kills Pee Sua Samut*

Just off the coast of Longka, cradled in the billows of the ocean, lies the hideous she-demon Pee Sua Samut. She is the guardian of the island, appointed by Totsagan himself, and, on seeing Hanuman, her eyes smoulder like coals and her great teeth clash. She springs up into the air, swinging her club and roaring.

The little monkey sees that words will be useless. Holding tightly onto his sword he enters her open mouth. Like a bumble bee in a cauldron, he flies round inside her head, and then in a flash he is down in the demon's stomach. A quick slash of his blade, and out he tumbles, none the worse for his adventure. Pee Sua Samut, without even knowing what has happened, collapses lifeless into the reddening waters, food for the fishes.

Hanuman wipes his sword nonchalantly. "So much for that," he says to himself, flying on.

17. *Hanuman kills Pee Sua Samut*

18. *Hanuman meets the hermit Nart*

On arriving at the island of Longka, Hanuman decides against going direct to the demon city and lands instead on the Solot Hills, where the hermit Nart lives.   Having taken on the appearance of an ordinary woodland monkey, Hanuman approaches the hermit and greets him diffidently.   He spins him a likely story to account for his leaving the forests of the mainland and then says with an assumed frankness, "To tell the truth, I've heard that Longka is a place where one can advance oneself and at the same time have some fun.   I must say, I hope to get a position with the demon king and perhaps earn myself a wife." The hermit laughs at the ingenuous monkey and tells him that if he has dealings with the demons of Longka, he will be lucky to escape with the hide on his back.   As to winning a wife—well, he just roars with laughter at the very idea.   Still chuckling to himself, the hermit tells Hanuman he may put up for the night at his nearby meditation cell, and advises him to change his mind about going to the demon city before the new day dawns.

19. *Hanuman bursts his cell*

More than a little nettled at the old man's condescension, Hanuman decides to play a trick on him.   Waiting until Nart is asleep, Hanuman enlarges his body and then calls out plaintively, "Wise one, here's a fine state of affairs.   I appeal to your generosity as a host, and what do I get? A cell so miserably small that it almost crushes me to death."   Nart, astonished at the size to which the monkey has grown, gets out his book of incantations, picks out an appropriate spell, and enlarges the cell.   No sooner has he settled to sleep, however, than Hanuman again increases his size and again calls out, "My good hermit, how can I be expected to get any rest in this miserable box?"   And once more, Nart enlarges the cell.   But when Hanuman tries the trick for a third time, and shatters the cell like an eggshell, the old man calls down a torrent of icy rain that soaks through Hanuman's pelt and makes his teeth chatter furiously.   Outsmarted, the monkey apologizes to the old man and, mollified, Nart kindles a magic fire to dry him out.   They then retire once more and sleep the rest of the night through.

20. *The leech sticks to Hanuman's chin*

Hermit Nart gets up before dawn and goes down to the pool to wash and prepare himself for meditation. Remembering the trouble his guest has given him during the night, he throws his stick into the pool and changes it into a leech.   Chuckling to himself, he goes away.   Hanuman is up with the lark.   Down he goes to the pool and ducks his face under the water to give it a good wash.   The leech fixes itself to his chin, and the Son of the Wind discovers that all his efforts to remove it are in vain.   In a panic he rushes to the hermit, throws himself at his feet and implores the old man to have pity on him.   Nart takes hold of the leech, mutters a spell and—presto, there is the stick in his hand.   He smiles down at Hanuman.   "Let that be a lesson, my good monkey," he says.

Hanuman takes his leave of the hermit and flies off, somewhat chastened, to the city of Longka.

19. *Hanuman bursts his cell*

20. *The leech sticks to Hanuman's chin*

21. *Hanuman flies to Longka*

THE BURNING OF LONGKA

21. Hanuman flies to Longka

22. Hanuman kills four watchmen

Very soon Hanuman sees the spires and walls of Longka city, and coming down to earth changes himself back into his forest form. Boldly he marches up to the main gate of the city and makes as if to enter. Four watchmen lounging at the gate call out to him sharply, "Where are you going, little monkey? Don't you know this is the city of the demon king? Be off with you to the forest, before we set about you."

"Little monkey!" chokes Hanuman, enraged at this incivility. "We'll see about that." He draws his sword and in short time so carves the four demons that their own mothers would not recognize them.

23. Hanuman kills the guardian of Longka

But no sooner has he put paid to the last of the watchmen than the guardian spirit of Longka, a monster with four faces—each uniquely horrible—and eight club-bearing arms leans out of the clouds and picks Hanuman up, sniffing him over.

"What have we got here," the demon mumbles to himself peering closely at the monkey. "Some new kind of rabbit, maybe." He suffers from myopia.

"Rabbit!" yells Hanuman furiously. "Know that I'm the invincible Hanuman, and meet your end." He wrenches himself free of the monster's grip and sets about him with his sword. In no time at all, Longka is without a guardian spirit. Wasting no ceremony on the matter, Hanuman picks up the body and throws it into the ocean.

"Rabbit!" he mutters.

24. Hanuman comes on Totsagan sleeping with Nang Monto

To avoid further encounters of this kind, Hanuman sings an incantation that puts the entire town to sleep. Unhindered, he is now able to pass on foot through the streets on his way to Totsagan's palace, where he expects to find Nang Seeda. Everywhere, in the streets, in the market and in their houses, the demons are stretched out asleep. The Son of the Wind enters the palace without difficulty, passing one gate after another until he comes to Totsagan's inner sanctum, and there, in the sleeping chamber—there is the demon king himself, and in his arms a woman of the most exquisite beauty. Enraged at the thought that Totsagan has been enjoying Phra Ram's wife, Hanuman growls and lifts his sword. But just at this moment, from somewhere out of the

23. *Hanuman kills the guardian of Longka*

24. *Hanuman comes on Totsagan sleeping with Nang Monto*

silence a gecko raises its warning cluck.   Hanuman pauses, lowers his sword, and looks closer.   The woman is Nang Monto, he sees now, the demon's legitimate wife.

The monkey continues the search for Nang Seeda, growing more and more impatient as the time passes. Having drawn a blank everywhere, he returns to the hermit's hut and asks Nart where he might find Phra Ram's queen.

"If you were not such an impatient monkey and didn't have such a high opinion of yourself, I might have told you where to find Nang Seeda in the first place," says Nart.   "As it happens, she is being kept in Totsagan's park, just outside the city walls."

Pausing only long enough to thank the hermit, Hanuman sweeps up into the air.   He quickly finds the park. Changing himself into a common monkey once more, he swings through the trees until he comes upon Nang Seeda.

---

25. *Demon torchbearers light Totsagan's way*
26. *Totsagan rides out to visit Nang Seeda*

Meanwhile, in Longka city, Totsagan has woken from his enchanted sleep.

Ever since he first saw Nang Seeda, he has suffered the scourging of an unrequited passion for her, which neither Nang Monto nor any other of his beautiful wives is able to assuage.   Every minute of the day is spent with the image of Nang Seeda before his eyes, while at night such sleep as he is able to snatch is haunted by her unattainable loveliness.

Now, such is his suffering, his very reason seems to be tottering.   Shouting, he rouses his women, calls up his bodyguard and charioteers, demands lights and food and drink.   The palace hums like an upset hive as the demons rush to fulfill the distracted king's demands.   In a little time he has been appareled in his most costly robes.   Mounted on his lion-drawn chariot and accompanied by a full retinue, he drives out to the park where Nang Seeda is confined.

The tumult of his arrival and the glitter of torchlight through the trees arrest Hanuman as he is about to disclose his presence to the sleepless and sorrowing Seeda.   The Son of the Wind takes in the situation in a flash and immediately swings himself into the branches of a tree, from which he can watch what happens and hear what is said without being seen.

---

27. *Totsagan pleads with Nang Seeda*

Dismissing his retinue, Totsagan approaches Nang Seeda, his heart tortured afresh at the sight of her.   Seating himself close to her, trying to speak in a calm voice, the demon king tells her of the pain he is suffering on her behalf.   Having summoned before her the picture of his torments, he pleads with her to pity him and give him

25. *Demon torchbearers light Totsagan's way*

26. *Totsagan rides out to visit Nang Seeda*

27. *Totsagan pleads with Nang Seeda*

peace.   Nothing that lies within his realm shall be denied her, he promises; let her ask for pearls from the bottom of the sea, or jewels from the center of the mountains, costly cloths from remote lands and scents from the deep forest, human beings as her servants, fabulous animals to draw her chariot—all these things shall be hers the moment she expresses a wish for them.   And more, far more than this shall be hers if she will only look upon him with the warm glance of compassion.   She shall be the queen of Longka, his first wife and joint ruler, with power equal to his.   There is nothing greater than this, except his life itself, that he can lay at her feet.

During this impassioned speech, Seeda has drawn herself away from the demon, filled with an unspeakable loathing and dread of the creature.   Now she masters her revulsion, and answers him briefly, calmly, "I am the wife of Phra Ram.   Either he will rescue me, or I shall die.   But a goddess shall never become the wife of a demon."

For a moment Totsagan continues to sit silently, like a man stunned.   Then he gets up and walks slowly away.   He mounts his chariot and looks back at Seeda.   "If you do not come to me soon of your own will," he says, "I shall come here with soldiers and take you by force."   With this newest image of her beauty and unwavering courage still before his eyes, the demon king drives back to his palace.

28. *Nang Seeda attempts to hang herself*

Thinking on the demon's parting words, Seeda decides that her position is hopeless.   She takes a cord from her breast cloth and, singing a plaintive love song to herself, walks down to the lotus pool.   The burden of her song is that although she must part from Phra Ram in this world, in the next they will be together forever.   She climbs a sturdy tree close to the pool and fastens one end of the cord to a limb.   With the other, she makes a noose and puts it around her delicate neck.   She takes her final look at the world of stars and waving branches and dim flowers and, with her last thoughts on Phra Ram, allows herself to fall.   The noose tightens, and Nang Seeda quickly becomes unconscious.

29. *Hanuman delivers his message to Nang Seeda*

But the Son of the Wind has followed her, puzzled as to what she is doing.   Now he leaps into the tree and unties the cord so that Nang Seeda falls unconcious to the ground.   As she recovers her senses, Hanuman prostrates himself at her feet, saying as he does so, "Look, I know I deserve all kinds of punishment for thwarting the will of the queen, but the fact of the matter is Phra Ram has given me a message to deliver to you and in the circumstances I don't see what else I could have done.   One way and another I should have been in trouble, so I hope you'll excuse me for interfering."   And still grumbling, he hands her the tokens and delivers his message as best he can.

Nang Seeda is by no means convinced that the tokens come from Phra Ram.   "I have only your word that

28. *Nang Seeda attempts to hang herself*

29. *Hanuman delivers his message to Nang Seeda*

you are one of Phra Narai's soldiers," she tells Hanuman. "But I don't recognize you, and these tokens could have been found by anyone. I'm afraid you are one of Totsagan's brood, saving me for your master's evil ends."

This is just what the shrewd monkey has been expecting her to say, so now he repeats Phra Ram's description of his first meeting with Seeda in Mitila town. Hearing it, Seeda is convinced and weeps.

Hanuman's embassy is now completed, but before leaving he urges Nang Seeda to accompany him. She refuses.

"It is ordained that Phra Ram must first slay the demons; then we shall be reunited. Tell him what I have said. And tell him that my love will wait for him."

And having said this, Nang Seeda returns sadly to her pavilion.

---

30. *Hanuman devastates Totsagan's park*

31. *Hanuman kills the watchmen of the park*

Hanuman decides to have some fun before leaving Longka. He runs through the park, breaking down fruit trees and uprooting bushes and shrubs and raising a terrible hullabaloo. The watchmen, after getting over their astonishment that a little white monkey can create so much havoc, fire arrows at him. Hanuman merely laughs and, when he tires of dodging their arrows, leaps down among them, doing terrible carnage with his sword. The survivors among the watchmen flee to Totsagan to tell him about the destructive intruder.

---

32. *Hanuman annihilates Totsagan's sons, the Pan Sahatsa Kuman*

Incensed, the demon king sends out his one thousand seven-faced sons, Pan Sahatsa Kuman, to deal with the monkey. They find Hanuman breaking the last of the trees in the devastated park and surround him.

"Little hooligan," they shout, "just what do you think you're doing?"

"Kindly step closer, my multi-faced friends, and Hanuman will show you," the Son of the Wind retorts.

At this impertinence, with much grinding of teeth, the Pan Sahatsa Kuman attack Hanuman. They might as well have set about a cloud in heaven. Hanuman is everywhere, snapping swords and catching arrows in midair, overturning chariots and choking lions. The demons he thumps, snaps, breaks, cracks, chokes, disembowels, chops into pieces and, in short, deals with them so violently that within a very brief space of time there is not one of the thousand left alive.

---

33. *Intorachit fires snake arrows at Hanuman*

When Totsagan hears what has happened, his grief and fury are boundless. Rushing from his Diamond Palace, he calls on his son Intorachit to destroy the monkey.

31. *Hanuman kills the watchmen of the park*

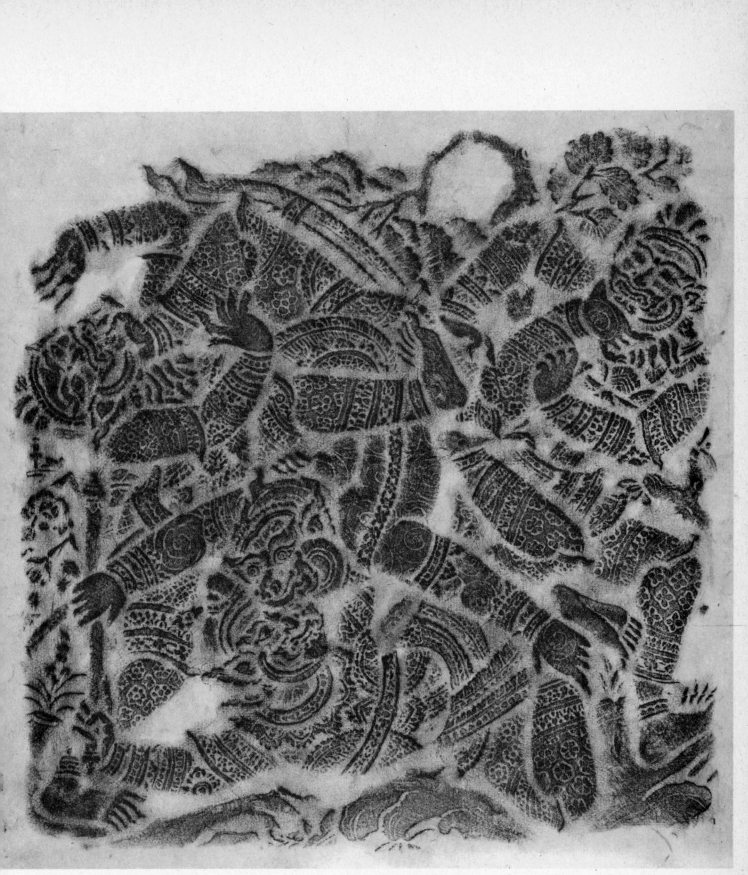

32. *Hanuman annihilates Totsagan's sons, the Pan Sahatsa Kuman*

34. *Hanuman is attacked by Intorachit's snake arrows*

33. *Intorachit fires snake arrows at Hanuman*

Now Intorachit is an extremely powerful warrior with the defeat of Phra In himself to his credit. Armed as he is with discus and bow, both weapons of miraculous powers, there is no reason to suppose he will be beaten.

Mounted in his war chariot and accompanied by his bodyguards, he drives out to the park. Hanuman, surrounded by corpses, is still there.

"Whoever you may be," says Intorachit, "prepare to die at my hands."

When he hears this, the Son of the Wind hoots with laughter. "This is all my own work," he says, indicating the broken trees and the dead bodies. "I did it without any help whatsoever. Do you imagine I'm going to tremble at your threats?"

By way of reply, Intorachit sends a hail of arrows at the mocking monkey. Hanuman catches them effortlessly, snaps them in half and throws them back at the demon's feet. Then he leaps up and plays havoc among Intorachit's retinue, overturning and smashing the chariots, killing the lions and putting the drivers to flight.

The son of the demon king is taken aback at this display. No ordinary monkey, he tells himself.

---

34. *Hanuman is attacked by Intorachit's snake arrows*
35. *Hanuman kills Intorachit's soldiers*
36. *Hanuman kills Intorachit's retainers*

The demon prince now selects his Nakabat arrow, bends his bow and fires it at Hanuman. The arrow changes in midair into hundreds of hissing snakes which entwine themselves about the monkey's limbs. If he wishes to do so Hanuman can easily free himself, but instead, after putting up token resistence—that is, killing the majority of the demon's bodyguard and personal retainers—he pretends to be bound fast by the serpents, and submits to Intorachit.

Proudly the demon prince orders his surviving warriors to bring the captive Hanuman before Totsagan.

---

37. *The executioner breaks a spear on Hanuman*

Totsagan is delighted with his son's victory. He praises Intorachit before the assembled demon court and then orders Hanuman to be taken to the place of execution. The court executioner is told to impale the monkey on an iron spear. With all due ceremony the executioner prepares to dispatch the meekly kneeling monkey, but to the astonishment of one and all, when he lunges at Hanuman with all his might the intended victim is unharmed, and the spear blade is snapped from its haft.

"Too bad," says Hanuman sympathetically, "try again."

The demons need no encouragement. A lance is quickly produced, and the executioner darts it at the monkey. It shatters to a hundred pieces.

"Tut-tut," says Hanuman.

35. *Hanuman kills Intorachit's soldiers*

36. *Hanuman kills Intorachit's retainers*

37. *The executioner breaks a spear on Hanuman*

A javelin is tried and shivered.   A trident makes no impression, while a mace, an axe and a club used successively strike sparks off Hanuman's diamond head but otherwise have no effect on the patient monkey.

As the demons debate what to try next, Hanuman springs up, showers the broken weapons on the bystanders and proceeds to make mincemeat of the executioner.   Just as suddenly he drops back to his knees, and with a most contrite expression says, "Please don't be discouraged.   Have another try."

38. *The attempt to pound Hanuman in a mortar fails*

Their conventional methods having failed, the demons now resort to pounding Hanuman to death in a mortar. For a while the diamond-hard monkey bears patiently with their attemps to make an impression on him, even encouraging them with calls of, "That's the stuff, friends, lay it on as hard as you can," and the like.   But suddenly he leaps out of the mortar, tears the pestle out of the hands of a demon and lays about him with it, cracking demon heads left and right.

39. *Hanuman tears the head off an elephant*

Thoroughly alarmed by this time, Totsagan consults with his courtiers to discover a sure method of killing the apparently invulnerable captive.   His chief adviser whispers in his ear.   Totsagan smiles and nods approval. Messengers hurry away at the demon's bidding, and all eyes turn to the door of the courtyard.

There is a wild trumpeting, the doors open, and in lumbers a huge bull elephant.   The beast is in musth and, seeing Hanuman in the center of the courtyard and goaded on by its mahout, bellows again wildly.   Hanuman calmly lays himself flat on the ground and permits the beast to trample and kneel on him to its heart's content. But when he tires of its ineffectual stomping, what does the Son of the Wind do?   Up he leaps with a great cry, hurls the mahout to death on the flags of the yard, and tears the head off the elephant with as little effort as if he were dealing with a fly.   He throws the bloody head among the courtiers.   "What next?" he enquires cheerfully.

40. *Totsagan sets fire to Hanuman*

Almost in despair, Totsagan has Hanuman brought before him.   "Is there no way to kill you?" he asks.

The cunning monkey thinks fast.   It is time to bring the business to an end and return to Phra Ram.   He assumes an expression of the utmost simplicity, bows before Totsagan and replies "Almost none, great king."

Totsagan takes heart at this.   "Almost none," he says.   "Then you must indeed be a powerful monkey. Tell me truthfully now, as one warrior to another, what is it that the gods have not protected you against?"

"Fire, my lord," says Hanuman promptly.   "If there's anything that can do for me, it's fire."

Totsagan gives a great laugh at the simplicity of the monkey, "Fetch me hay and fibers and cotton," he says, "and jars of palm oil."

38. *The attempt to pound Hanuman in a mortar fails*

39. *Hanuman tears the head off an elephant*

The materials are brought. The demon orders that Hanuman be securely bound in the materials, which are then thoroughly soaked with oil. Totsagan takes his diamond spear.

"Now, monkey," he says, "we shall see what you are made of." And with one great blow of his spear against Hanuman's flinty hide, he turns him into a blazing torch.

41. Hanuman sets fire to Longka

Hanuman waits until the flames have taken a good hold on the materials around him and then leaps over the courtiers and into the palace. He flies from chamber to chamber, stopping briefly here and there to start a blaze before moving on, the demons always one move behind and hampered in their efforts to capture the monkey by their attempts to quench the fires he has started. Within a matter of minutes the whole palace is ablaze, so Hanuman turns his attention to the city. Soon Longka is a sea of flame.

Well satisfied with his work, Hanuman flies over to the sea and plunges in. When he emerges he is pleased to see that the flames are extinguished—all that is except those licking at the end of his tail. He plunges it into the water again and again, but still it burns. Desperate, he flies to the hut of the hermit Nart, throwing himself prostrate before him and begging breathlessly to be told how to put out the fire.

The hermit looks at him sourly. "You're clever enough to set fire to Longka and fill the island with pestilential smoke. How is it you can't help yourself?" he asks.

"This is no ordinary fire," says Hanuman. "It was started by Totsagan's diamond spear."

"If that's the case," says the hermit, "you can soon put it right."

> "Listen hard and I will tell
> How you can quench your fiery tail.
> Take its end and without fail
> Place it in the little well."

Hanuman understands immediately. He sticks his burning tail in his mouth and pinches his nostrils. The flame goes out at once. Hanuman throws himself gratefully before the hermit once more, thanks him, and then flies back over the ocean to his waiting companions, and then on to Phra Ram's camp.

42. Totsagan flees burning Longka with his wives

Totsagan's first thought is for his wives. Hurrying through the blazing palace he breaks into the women's quarters and drags out the panic-stricken Nang Monto and his other women. Mounting his cloud chariot Butsabok, he flees with them to Mount Satana, leaving his hapless subjects to fend for themselves. Many perish miserably in the flames.

40. *Totsagan sets fire to Hanuman*

41. *Hanuman sets fire to Longka*

42. *Totsagan flees burning Longka with his wives*

The other nobles follow their king's leadership and, giving up their futile attemps to save the city, flee to Mount Satana. Pipeck, the king's brother—a demon skilled in clairvoyance and the arts of astrology—and Intorachit, his son, succeed in escaping the doomed city.

Kumpagan, however, the Regent of Longka and another brother of Totsagan, is almost killed. He is a prodigious eater, and a sleeper without equal. At a sitting he not infrequently devours a whole flock of sheep and a herd of cattle, washing them down with enough wine to float a large ship. Then it is his custom to sleep off the effects of this snack, a nap to him being a couple of months long. The burning of Longka takes place during one of his sleeps, and it is only through the devotion of his wives that he is woken and hurried out of the city—belching and muttering thickly to himself—while there is still time.

In the safety of the folds of Mount Satana the court assembles itself about Totsagan, who immediately confers with his advisers on what to do about the destruction of Longka. The advisers suggest that messengers are first sent to Phra Piroon, the Rain God, to ask him to put out the fire. As Phra Piroon is an ally of Totsagan, he gladly causes a torrent of rain to fall on Longka, which puts out the flames. This prompt action cannot save the buildings, but some of the materials can be used in the reconstruction of the city.

As to the creation of a new capital, the advisers remind Totsagan that he has credit at the court of heaven and suggest he petition the gods Isuan and Witsanukam—the latter being the heavenly architect—to carry out the rebuilding for him.

43. *Pipeck and Intorachit flee with their wives*

44. *Kumpagan is saved by his wives*

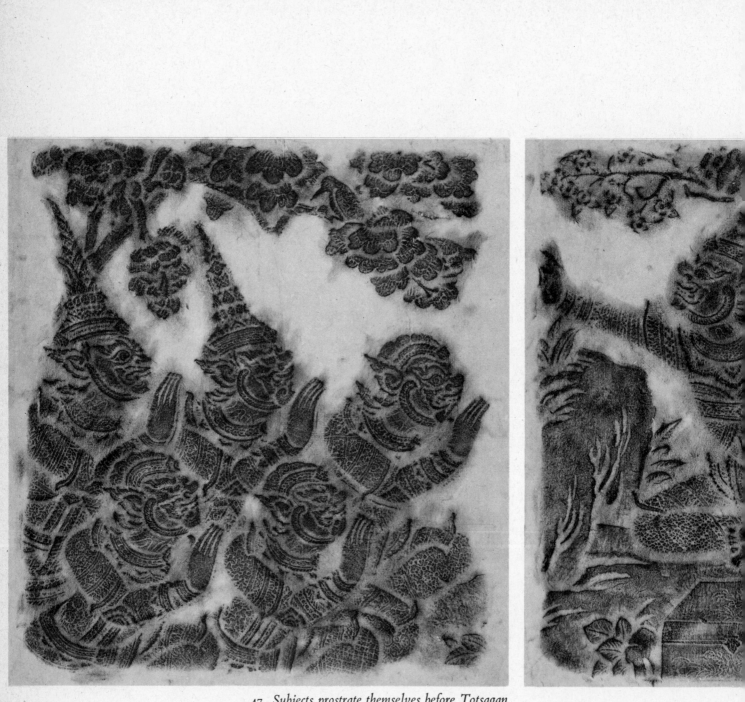

47. *Subjects prostrate themselves before Totsagan*

100

Totsagan orders the rebuilding of Longka

45. *Courtiers listen to Totsagan*

101

48. *Messengers fly to Phra Isuan*

49. *Phra In and Phra Witsanukam rebuild Longka*

Without delay two messengers fly to the heavenly court and after due scrutiny at the gate are admitted to the royal and divine presence. Prostrating themselves before Phra Isuan, they tell him the whole story and beg him to rebuild Longka for their master. Isuan dismisses them and discusses the matter with his closest advisers. They point out to him that while Totsagan is by no means as close to the heavenly king as Phra Ram, it would not be wise to turn down his request out of hand. In the first place, this might upset the balance of power between Phra Ram and Totsagan, with unforeseeable results. And then, the demon king might well turn to other courts for aid and, having had his city rebuilt by them, never again pay to the heavenly court of Isuan the tribute that it should rightly receive. The consequence is that Phra Isuan summons the messengers and tells them that he will undertake to provide the aid Totsagan has requested.

The two gods Phra In and Phra Witsanukam rebuild the demon city, and within a matter of days, so quickly and expertly do the two gods go about their task, Longka stands again even more splendid and beautiful than it was before the fire.

50. *Totsagan tells Pipeck his dreams*

51. *Pipeck interprets Totsagan's dreams*

Shortly after the reconstruction of Longka, Totsagan has two ominous dreams, which he calls on his brother, Pipeck, a demon with skill in such arts, to interpret.

"A white vulture came flying from the East," says Totsagan. "It crossed the ocean on powerful wings and landed in Longka's marketplace. A black vulture came flying from the West. Seeing it, the white bird climbed high above the newcomer and then swooped. The two vultures clashed and with flashing talons and curved beaks fought until the feathers flew. The black bird fell vanquished and died. As it did so, I became aware that it was of the demons' party."

"Then came the second dream," Totsagan continues. "A demon carried in his hand half a coconut shell, filled with oil, in which a wick floated. A beautiful woman lit the wick. The fire spread from the wick to the nutshell and then to the demon's hand and on until the whole of the demon's body was consumed by the flames."

"Tell me, brother Pipeck, what it is these dreams mean."

Pipeck, who has been noting down occult symbols during this narration, now consults his board.

48. *Messengers fly to Phra Isuan*

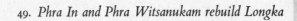

49. *Phra In and Phra Witsanukam rebuild Longka*

51. *Pipeck interprets Totsagan's dreams*

50. *Totsagan tells Pipeck his dreams*

"The interpretation is not hard to arrive at," he says. "The white vulture is Phra Ram, and the black yourself, King Totsagan. The first dream means that Phra Ram will defeat you in battle. The beautiful woman in the second dream in Nang Seeda. It warns of the downfall of your kingly self, of Longka and of the demon race through Nang Seeda." So says Pipeck.

Totsagan, displeased at this interpretation, asks, "How may these things be circumvented?" And his brother replies, "Only by the return of Nang Seeda."

For a moment the king is speechless. He thinks of the suffering the pursuit of the goddess has caused him and the misfortune it has brought his kingdom, and his anger rises. "Return Seeda!" he says. "These are the words of a traitor."

52. Pipeck flees Longka

Pipeck throws himself at Totsagan's feet, appeals to him as a brother born of the same mother to heed his warning. But the demon king, his rage mounting by the moment, draws his sword and beats his brother from his presence, proclaiming him outlawed and setting Kumpagan and Intorachit to hunt him down. His brother's property, including his wife Dreechada and his daughter Benyagai, is seized by the king.

Pipeck flees Longka, escaping only with his life.

53. Nilek captures Pipeck
54. Pipeck is led before Phra Ram

The outlawed Pipeck can see no possibility for himself but to offer his services to Phra Ram. Having flown over the sea and arrived on the mainland, he searches diligently for the camp of the monkeys. As he is doing so, he stumbles on a foraging party under the leadership of the black monkey general Nilek, who immediately takes him to be a spy and orders his capture.

Pipeck's protestations are useless, and he is led into the monkey camp with his neck in a halter. There he is brought before the commander in chief, who, realizing what a prize they have captured, orders him to be taken before Phra Ram.

55. Phra Ram and Phra Lak hear Pipeck's story
56. Pipeck relates his story

Pipeck pays his respects to the royal brothers and tells them the sad story of his banishment. He explains that he has come of his own free will to the monkey camp to beg to be taken into the service of Phra Ram to fight in the campaign against his brother Totsagan. It requires very little thought for the brothers to see the advantages of having a demon in their ranks, and after a minimum of discussion it is decided that Pipeck is to

52. Pipeck flees Longka

53. *Nilek captures Pipeck*

110

54. *Pipeck is led before Phra Ram*

56. *Pipeck relates his story*

55. *Phra Ram and Phra Lak hear Pipeck's story*

113

act as the royal soothsayer. Furthermore, as he is the possessor of great occult powers, it is thought fitting that he shall be the guardian of the blessed water in which Ram's Promat arrow is lustrated.

57. The monkey army assembles
58. Pipeck swears the oath of allegiance

When this has been decided, the entire monkey army is paraded, with the generals in the forefront and the rank and file drawn up all round. Before this host, Pipeck swears an oath of allegiance to Phra Ram, promising to serve him faithfully until Longka is defeated and Nang Seeda is recovered.

Following these ceremonies, Sukreep seeks out Pipeck and after an exchange of compliments tells him that they should be friends.

"We have a melancholy history in common," he explains. "At one time, I had an enemy who did me wrong and tried to bring about my death. This enemy was Palee, King of Keetkin, and he was my elder brother. Your worst enemy is similarly your brother, Totsagan of Longka, who also seeks your life. Thus our fates are similar. Let us therefore swear to be friends for the rest of our lives."

And so Pipeck, deprived of home, friends and family, forges new bonds of loyalty among strangers.

59. Phra Ram calls a council of war
60. The monkey generals receive their orders

By this time Phra Ram is thinking of pushing on with his campaign against Longka. He calls a council of war of his monkey generals and orders them to carry out military maneuvers with their troops, so that he can see just how they will fare against the warlike demons under Totsagan's command, and, at the same time, impress his new ally with the forces under his banner.

61. Pipeck and Sukreep take up their positions
62. The monkeys engage in mock battle

Sukreep issues his orders, and then leads Pipeck to an eminence from which they can best view the maneuvers. The army divides into two forces, which then lock in mock battle. It is an extraordinary sight that Pipeck witnesses. Some of the monkeys dart up into the air, from where they rain down rocks on each other, or engage in desperate hand to hand combat; others fight on the sea, lashing the surface into a tornado of foam; yet others create artificial fire, or blot out the sun, or call up tempests—performing, in short, marvels without name or number. The noise of this battle shakes the earth to its foundations and rises as high as the fourth heaven, where the angels hide their eyes in fear and flee behind the stars for protection. Pipeck is highly impressed.

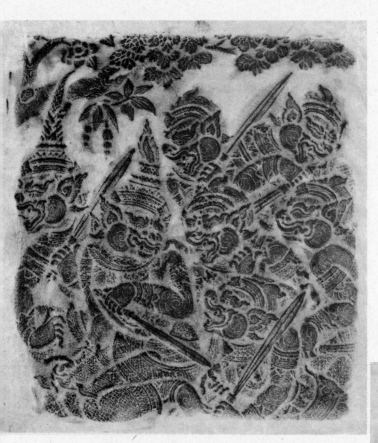

57. *The monkey army assembles*

58. *Pipeck swears the oath of allegiance*

60. *The monkey generals receive their orders*

59. *Phra Ram calls a council of war*

61. *Pipeck and Sukreep take up their positions*

118

62. *The monkeys engage in mock battle*

63. *A spy watches the mock battle*

The tumult of the monkey maneuver reaches as far as Longka and, hearing it, Totsagan orders one of his demon subjects to find out just what is happening.

The demon, Sukrasan by name, changes himself into a falcon and flies high over the sea to the mainland. Coming to the battlefield, he finds himself a convenient rock face and observes what is going on closely. In fact, so closely is he following the feats the monkeys are performing that he relaxes the concentration necessary to maintain his guise and tumbles to the bottom of the cliff.

Not much the worse for his fall, however, Sukrasan changes himself again, this time into a monkey, and as such mingles with the soldiers of Phra Ram's army.

64. *Hanuman changes himself into a mountain and catches the spy*

Sukrasan's new form is not good enough to pass the penetrating eye of Pipeck. The soothsayer informs Sukreep, who passes the word on to Phra Ram, that the battle is being observed by a spy. Hanuman is summoned and ordered to capture him.

Now, while Peepeck with his special gifts is able to pick out the imposter immediately, Hanuman finds it much harder. He flies round the battlefield for some time, but gets so confused by the ceaseless movement of the monkeys that he gives a great howl, bringing them all to a standstill, and at that moment transforms himself into a mountain encircling the entire army.

"Now then," he says, "you will pass through my hands, one by one, until I find the demon. And when I find him . . . " and here he utters threats so horrifying that Sukrasan can hardly control his trembling limbs. He wishes most heartily he could find a way of escaping, but as there seems no choice but to pass through Hanuman's hands, he joins the waiting line of monkeys and trusts that his appearance is sufficiently convincing to pass muster. However, at the moment when it is his turn to be lifted up and sniffed at and examined closely by the Son of the Wind, Sukrasan is so terrified that he inadvertantly changes back into his original form, and the game is up.

65. *Phra Ram is informed of the spy's capture*
66. *Sukreep, Pipeck and Hanuman inform Phra Ram of the spy's capture*

Phra Ram is informed of the spy's capture. After conferring with his brother, he orders that Sukrasan shall not be put to death. Instead he shall receive only the mild punishment of a beating and then be allowed to return to Longka. In this way Phra Ram not only demonstrates his clemency but is sure the news of the power and determination of his army shall reach the ears of his adversary.

63. *A spy watches the mock battle*

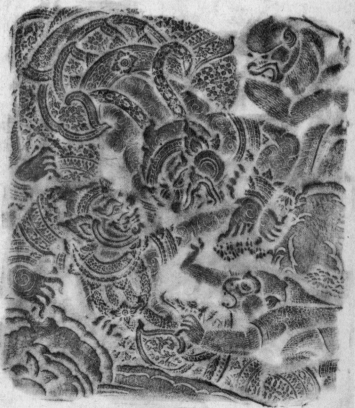

64. *Hanuman changes himself into a mountain and catches the spy*

121

66. *Sukreep, Pipeck and Hanuman inform Phra Ram of the spy's capture*

65. *Phra Ram is informed of the spy's capture*

And so the unfortunate Sukrasan is handed over to the monkeys. They strip him and truss him securely to a couple of boughs cut from a nearby tree. His forehead is branded with a hot iron, so that he shall always bear witness to his ignominious capture by Phra Ram's army. Then the monkeys thoroughly beat him, laying it on with such a will that Sukrasan begins to wish he had been put to death. Finally, as a last mark of disgrace, his eyebrows are shaved, and he is hissed out of the monkey camp and sent flying—more dead than alive—on his way back to Longka.

67. *Sukrasan is beaten*

68. *Sukrasan flies back to Longka*

69. *Totsagan orders Benyagai to assume the appearance of Nang Seeda*

When Sukrasan returns with the news of Phra Ram's warlike preparations, Totsagan is deeply disturbed. He calls together a council of ministers and asks them what course of action they advise. It is decided that Phra Ram must be diverted from his intended campaign against Longka.

The demon king summons Benyagai, Pipeck's daughter, and gives her the following instructions. Using the magic powers learned from her father, she is to assume the form and appearance of Nang Seeda. Having done so, she must then be found, apparently dead, in the vicinity of the monkey camp. Totsagan tells her that if Phra Ram is deceived and decides to call off his campaign against Longka as having no further point, she, Benyagai, may expect to be suitably rewarded.

70. *Benyagai goes by chariot to see Nang Seeda*
71. *Benyagai discusses the situation with her mother, Dreechada*

Benyagai is terrified when she hears this plan. She knows that she can expect no mercy from the monkeys if her deception is uncovered, but she is equally sure that her uncle will deal with her ruthlessly if she refuses to do his bidding. Alone and friendless at the court, she has no choice but to give her assent. Weeping, Benyagai mounts the chariot that Totsagan puts at her disposal and is taken to the park where Nang Seeda is held prisoner.

On the way, she stops to tell her mother Dreechada of the mission that Totsagan has thrust on her. Still weeping, Benyagai asks her what she should do.

The sight of her daughter's unhappiness brings home sharply to Dreechada the hopelessness of their position, and she is unable to restrain her own tears. She counsels Benyagai to obey the orders of the demon king and to pray to the gods for their protection.

72. *Benyagai studies Nang Seeda*

At the entrance to the park Benyagai leaves the chariot and seeks out Nang Seeda on foot. Having enquired the way of one of the demon ladies attending Ram's wife, she arrives at the pavilion where Seeda, sad and solitary, spends her days.

Throwing herself at the feet of the lovely queen, Benyagai sobs out the story of her father's banishment and her own plight at the court of the demon king, giving Seeda to understand that being in a position almost as unfortunate as the captive queen, her sympathies lie outside the court of which she is a member; and this, indeed,

69. *Totsagan orders Benyagai to assume the appearance of Nang Seeda*

70. *Benyagai goes by chariot to see Nang Seeda*

71. *Benyagai discusses the situation with her mother, Dreechada*

is almost the truth of the matter. But even while she is telling her story and arousing Nang Seeda's compassion, she is imprinting the very image of Ram's wife on her memory. By the time she takes her leave, promising to return to talk with Seeda whenever she has the opportunity, every particular of Nang Seeda's person—her features, her form, the texture and coloring of her skin, the arch of her brow and the tint of her lovely eyes— every item is held fast within the young demon's memory.

Having transformed herself into Nang Seeda's double, Benyagai reappears before the demon king. Totsagan, astounded at this apparition, and thinking that the woman he has desired so long has come to surrender herself to him, descends from the throne, and raises her from her knees. Embracing her, Totsagan promises again that she shall become the mistress of half his possessions. When Benyagai is able to free herself from his arms, she changes back to her original form. For a moment Totsagan is disappointed and angry but quickly recovers himself. "My dear niece," he gloats, "if I am pained by this ruse, how much more the humans are going to suffer when they see you."

Exulting at the prospect of Phra Ram's pain, he sends Benyagai on her way.

---

73. *Phra Ram and Phra Lak weep over "Seeda's" body*
74. *Sukreep, Pipeck and Hanuman express their grief*

In the early morning, when the sun has not yet risen above the trees and the air is still cool, Phra Ram comes down to the sea to bathe.* As always, his thoughts are with his absent wife, and to ease the pain of separation, he sings a love song softly to himself as he goes, promising that the days until their reunion shall be few.

He sees a body—that of an exquisitely beautiful woman—lying as if cast up on the shore. Going closer, he realizes—with a horror that no words can describe—that the corpse is that of his wife. He sinks to his knees beside the body, tenderly lifts it from the ground, and calls in a broken voice for his brother Lak.

Hearing the sound of voices raised in lamentation, Hanuman hurries down to the shore, followed by Sukreep and Pipeck. "This is what comes of your folly in Longka," Phra Ram upbraids Hanuman. "If you had not enraged the demon king, Nang Seeda would still be alive." At first Hanuman is too shocked to speak, but soon his eyes take in two discrepancies that have escaped the others, and his quicksilver brain reaches a conclusion.

"With all due respect," he says, "you are weeping in vain. That is not Nang Seeda. Look at the currents of this strait. They flow towards Longka, so how could they have brought this body here. And then I never saw a corpse that didn't show some sign of disorder or corruption. It's my opinion this is another of Totsagan's tricks. Let us burn the corpse and see what happens."

---

* As it is neither Hindu nor Buddhist practice to bathe in the sea, it seems that two episodes have been compressed here; in one of these Phra Ram went down to perform his ablutions at the river, and, in the other, Benyagai's body was washed up on the seashore. The texts are ambiguous on this point.

72. *Benyagai studies Nang Seeda*

74. *Sukreep, Pipeck and Hanuman express their grief*

132

73. *Phra Ram and Phra Lak weep over "Seeda's" body*

At Hanuman's command the monkeys build a funeral pyre and place the "corpse" on it. The pyre is lit and the flames swiftly lick through the dry wood. Up to this point Benyagai has played her part perfectly, but this is more than she can bear. With a shriek she changes into her own form and flies up into the air, intending to to make her escape.

This is exactly what Hanuman has been expecting. In no time at all he is up in the air and in pursuit. Poor Benyagai is no match for him in speed, and still less in strength. Hanuman overtakes her, siezes her by her long and flowing tresses, and drags her unceremoniously back to the camp.

76. *Benyagai is interrogated by Sukreep*

An impromptu court of enquiry is convened, with commander in chief Sukreep as its presiding officer. Benyagai sees that there can be no further point in deception and divulges her errand and her identity.

"I am Benyagai, daughter of Pipeck, Prince of Longka," she says. "Totsagan, the demon king, imposed this undertaking on me, and I had no choice but to obey him."

Phra Ram summons his soothsayer and commands him to pass judgement on his daughter. In tears—for demons no less than human kind are subject to paternal devotion—Pipeck admits that there can be no other punishment for his daughter's deception than death. Phra Ram is deeply touched, both by the demon's suffering and by his loyalty. "Come now," he says, "she is your daughter, the comfort of your old age. She shall live. Indeed, she shall return to Longka and tell our adversary of his newest defeat."

Hanuman is told to see Benyagai safely on her way to Longka. One might as well imagine that water will not dissolve sugar as expect the gallant monkey not to exercise his charms upon a lovely woman. They have flown no great distance before his soft words, warm looks and ardent caresses awaken passion in Benyagai's slender form. Somewhere before the Hematiwan Mountains they sink to the mossy floor of the forest, where only the nodding flowers and the shy beasts of the woodland are their witnesses, and embrace.

Some time later, Benyagai arrives back at Longka and tells Totsagan of the failure of her mission. Disappointed though he is, the king gives her a regal reward.

Hanuman, too, is a little late returning to camp. The generals ask him if he had trouble on the way.

"Quite the contrary," says Hanuman.

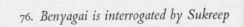

76. *Benyagai is interrogated by Sukreep*

78. *Sukreep, Hanuman and Nilapat receive their orders*

77. *Phra Ram orders the building of the causeway to Longka*

Now that the army is ready to move on Longka, Phra Ram assembles his staff officers and tells them that a causeway must be built between the mainland and Longka island so that the army and all its baggage and supplies can be taken safely across the strait. He orders Sukreep to supervise the operation, while Hanuman and Nilapat, with the other monkeys of the army as their laborers, are chosen to carry out the construction work.

Glad to be away from the camp again, Hanuman flies blithely down to the strait with his companions. He might perhaps be less happy if he knew what his workmate Nilapat is thinking. The fact is that the black monkey has been nursing a grudge against the Son of the Wind since the time Hanuman abducted his foster father King Chompoo in order to bring him before Phra Ram. The great Chompoo readily forgave Hanuman on learning that Phra Ram wanted to enlist his aid in the campaign against the demons, but Nilapat has been brooding ever since over what he feels was an affront to his honor as Chompoo's personal guard. So far he has nursed his resentment in secret, but now, flying down to the Longka strait, he promises himself he will pay off his score with Hanuman.

While the Sukreep goes off to attend to other business, the two monkeys prepare for work. "I suggest you stand in the water, brother Hanuman," says the sly Nilapat, "while I toss you the rocks from the mainland."

"Fair enough," says Hanuman, "but mind you throw the rocks straight and at reasonable intervals. It's going to be hot work out there."

Nilapat laughs gleefully to himself as he flies to the nearby Himaphan Mountains. "This is going to be fun," he says to himself. On the side of the mountain he gathers together a pile of rocks the size of small pavilions. "Ready?" he shouts to Hanuman, who is standing out in the water. "Let's begin." And he takes rocks and throws them across to the Son of the Wind, at first at a reasonable speed, but gradually faster and faster and closer and closer together, so that Hanuman has to work at furious speed to keep himself from being buried beneath them. Even though he can use both hands independently of each other, plucking the rocks out of the air and placing them in position on the sea bed, his pelt is soaked with sweat by the time Nilapat has run through his supply. "You'll be needing a rest, I suppose," shouts Nilapat maliciously. "Not in the least," Hanuman bawls back. "Just let's change places and I'll be ready to continue immediately." But to himself he growls, "And then we'll see about playing games."

---

82. *Hanuman collects rocks*

83. *Hanuman attaches the rocks to his body*

84. *Hanuman unloads the rocks onto Nilapat*

Hanuman flies to the mountainside and quickly gathers together rocks of a suitable size, which he attaches to the hairs of his body. Up he shoots into the air and heads out over the strait. "Catch this lot then, partner," he shouts down to Nilapat, who, startled to hear Hanuman's voice from overhead, looks up to see what appears to be a mountain flying directly above him.

"What?... One at a time, brother, one at a time," Nilapat quavers, but before he can utter another word, Hanuman shakes himself like a wet dog, and down come the rocks with a roar. Like a lone pine before an avalanche, like an ant under a landslide, Nilapat is engulfed and disappears. It is a full minute before he can pick himself off the bed of the sea and reemerge above the waves, wet, bruised and seething with rage. Hanuman is helpless with laughter at the sight of him.

Nilapat is nearly beyond words. He lurches up into the air, screaming as he does so, "That's just the kind of behavior I might have expected from a blackguard of your sort. But now I'm going to teach you a lesson you'll never forget."

---

85. *Sukreep comes between Hanuman and Nilapat*

The two monkeys clash with a noise like thunder. Hanuman is quick to see that Nilapat means business and lashes out with both feet to send the enraged animal crashing against Mount Jakrawan. Nilapat, winded but undeterred, springs back at Hanuman and, with eyes glowing like coals, deals the Son of the Wind a blow that sends him hurtling to the ground. The concussion of his fall topples trees for miles around. "If that's the the way things are," says Hanuman between his teeth, "see how you like the taste of cold steel," and the two monkeys snatch up their swords and square away, circling and feinting, looking for an opening to get in a deadly thrust. They are hard at it, cutting and thrusting, their blades clashing and striking sparks from each other, when Sukreep comes between them, shouting in his authoritative voice for them to put up their weapons and commanding the lesser monkeys to hold them apart. Even so, it is quite five minutes before the furious antagonists have stopped cursing and glaring at each other, and longer before they can be safely released and led separately back to the camp.

But the matter does not stop there.

79. *Sukreep, Hanuman and Nilapat on their way to the strait*

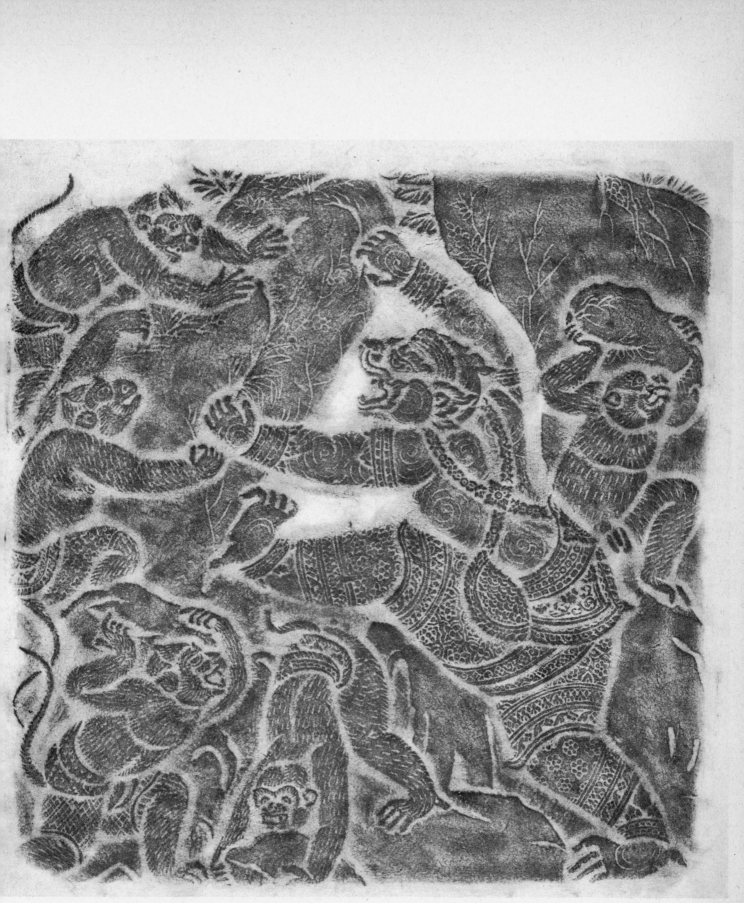

80. *Nilapat collects rocks for the causeway*

81. *Nilapat throws the rocks at Hanuman*

82. *Hanuman collects rocks*

144

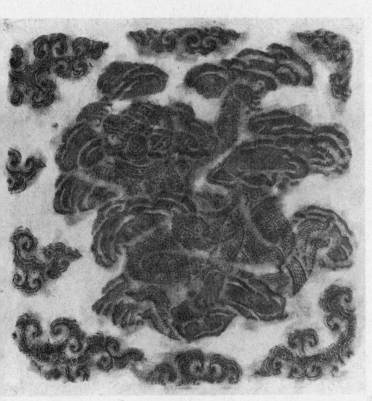

83. *Hanuman attaches the rocks to his body*

84. *Hanuman unloads the rocks onto Nilapat*

145

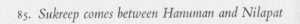

85. *Sukreep comes between Hanuman and Nilapat*

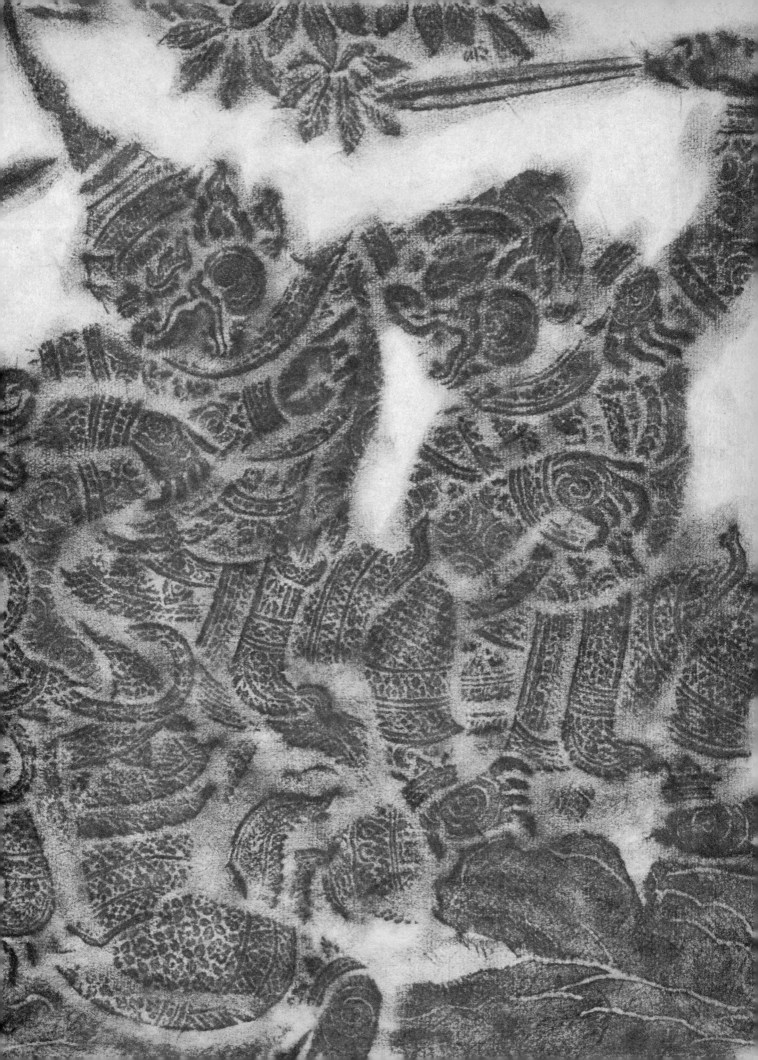

87. *Nilapat, Pipeck, Hanuman and Sukreep attend Phra Ram's judgement*

86. *Phra Ram pronounces judgement on the two monkeys*

88. *Phra Ram pronounces judgement on the two monkeys*

87. *Nilapat, Pipeck, Hanuman and Sukreep attend Phra Ram's judgement*

The noise of their conflict has come to the ears of Phra Ram. Angry that his own officers should be fighting when so much is still to be done, he orders his brother to bring the offenders before him.

Each of the monkeys is brought to Phra Ram under escort and tells his version of the story behind the conflict. So furious do they both become again that their voices rise, and if it were not for their guards they would again be at each other's throats. Phra Ram, however, commands them to be silent and reminds them that the punishment for their crime is not less than death. Hearing this, the monkeys tremble. Sukreep, however, intercedes with Phra Ram, pointing out that the morale of the army might be affected by the loss of so powerful an ally as Hanuman, while Chompoo himself could hardly remain well disposed toward them if his foster son were executed.

Having considered this advice, Phra Ram pronounces judgement.

"Nilapat is to return to Chompoo in disgrace, another general from the monkey city taking his place. Hanuman is to complete the building of the causeway to Longka island within seven days—or his life shall be forfeit," he decrees.

88. *Hanuman collects boulders for the causeway*

89. *The monkeys throw the rocks into the strait*

90. *Sukreep advises Hanuman to examine the seabed*

Hanuman gets to work on the causeway without further delay. For two days all goes well, and the road to Longka grows out into the strait. Under Sukreep's direction, and with Hanuman's superhuman example to spur them on, the lesser monkeys redouble their efforts, and it seems certain that the construction will be finished before the end of the appointed time. On the third day, however, a curious thing happens. All progress stops. The monkeys continue to hurl their rocks into the water, but not one inch further forward does the causeway advance. It is as if the materials are being hurled into a bottomless gulf. Conscious that time is passing, Hanuman works even faster, but even so, by the end of the third day the monkeys have nothing to show for their labor.

Sukreep, perturbed by this state of affairs, takes his nephew to one side. "Hanuman, my boy," he says, "something is wrong here. I suspect our friend Totsagan is up to his tricks. If you value your life, you'll take my advice and dive down there below the green waves and see why our work is being held up."

Hanuman is only too pleased to take his uncle's advice. The laborious business of carting stones is not much in his line, and he thinks a bit of diversion will come in nicely. He grips his sword firmly, and having saluted Sukreep, the Son of the Wind kicks up his heels and dives neatly under the turbulent waves.

88. *Hanuman collects boulders for the causeway*

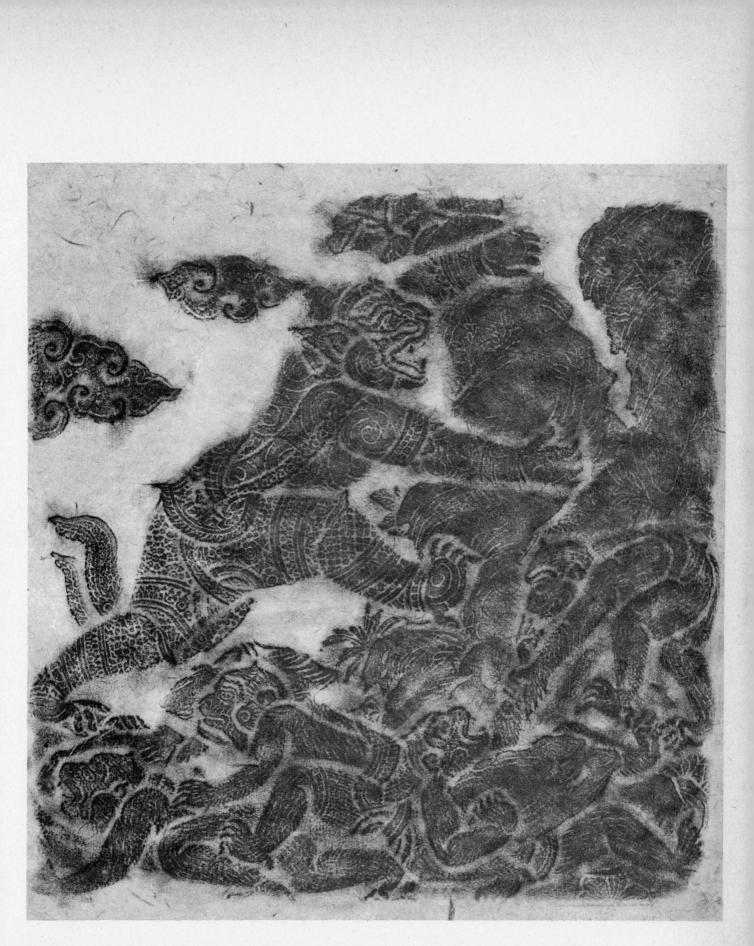

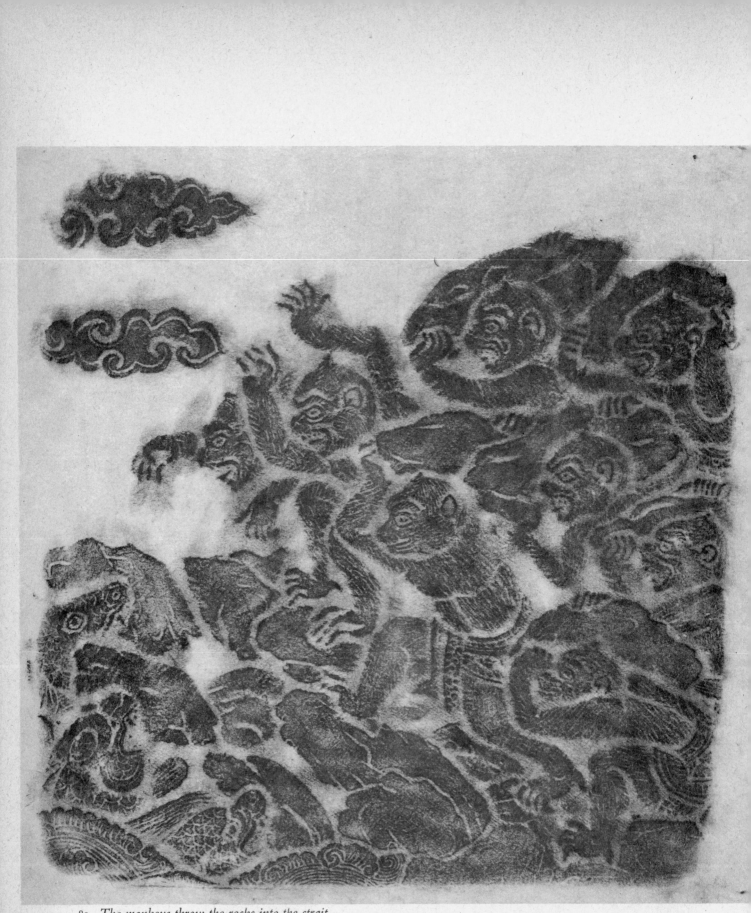

89. *The monkeys throw the rocks into the strait*

90. *Sukreep advises Hanuman to examine the seabed*

91. *Hanuman discovers and catches a mermaid*

When his eyes have accustomed themselves to the green and murky light below the surface, Hanuman is astonished to find the water alive with fishes. Schools, shoals, swarms of the glittering creatures flash here and there, and with a shock of indignation the Son of the Wind realizes that while those swimming towards the causeway have empty jaws, those swimming away from it bear stones, rocks and even boulders, each according to its size, fixed firmly between their teeth.

"Now then," roars Hanuman, brandishing his sword, "be off with you, or you'll all end up over a hot fire."

At the sight and sound of this furry monster, the fishes with one accord turn tail and flee, vanishing in a flash of scales. To his annoyance, Hanuman sees that one fish—is it a fish though?—has disobeyed his command, and hovers resolutely some way off in the mistiness. "Now I'm really getting angry," he mutters to himself and streaks towards the figure, his sword raised for the kill. As he comes closer his arm falls, his resolution deserts him, and he gapes with surprise. Facing him, her tail twitching this way and that with outrage, is the most exquisite mermaid he has ever seen—golden-bodied and with the tail of a fish, but in all other respects a model of femininity.

This lovely creature is really rather frightened at the sight of the powerful monkey, but she doesn't intend to show it. With yet another whisk of her tail that stirs up a little whirlwind of sand, she says angrily, "How dare you frighten my subjects like that. I'll have you know that you are dealing with Supanna Matcha, daughter of Totsagan of Longka and Queen of the Ocean. From this moment you are my prisoner."

"Prisoner!" shouts Hanuman, and doubles up with laughter. "You are MY prisoner," and in a flash he leaps at her. Supanna Matcha eludes him and is off like lightning. But, fast as she is, the Son of the Wind is faster and very quickly has her in his arms.

92. *Hanuman makes love to Supanna Matcha*

Whatever Hanuman's intentions in pursuing her, once she is in his arms he has only one thought in mind—to take not her life but her love. Supanna Matcha at first weeps and wails and laments her lot, but slowly, skillfully, passionately, the resourceful monkey kindles the fire in her veins that burns in his own, and it is not long before, many fathoms down on the soft seabed, they are tasting the delights of love.

Later the enamored mermaid queen tells Hanuman the whole story. Totsagan's watchmen had seen and reported to the king the rapid construction of the causeway to Longka, and the demon king had sent instructions to his daughter to ensure that the monkeys' work was brought to nothing. So she had assembled her sea minions and directed them to carry away the rocks as soon as they were thrown into the sea. That is what they had been doing when Hanuman had come.

91. *Hanuman discovers and catches a mermaid*

The Son of the Wind tells her his side of the story, or at least as much of it as he considers suitable. Preening himself, he explains that he is one of Phra Ram's most important generals, and describes how the conflict between Ram and her father started.

Having told her of his quarrel with Nilapat, and Phra Ram's decree, he makes it clear that his life depends on his completing the causeway within a further four days. If her subjects continue to carry away the rocks, he explains, he will certainly be executed. Supanna Matcha assures him that her subjects, far from hindering his work, will replace those rocks they have taken away. And so, with many a long-drawn-out sigh between them, they part.

This interlude has consequences for the golden-bodied Goddess of the Sea—and indeed for Hanuman—that will be related later.

93. *Phra Ram rides over the causeway to Longka*
94. *The monkey generals salute Phra Ram*

Greatly refreshed by his underwater excursion, and secretly aided as he is by the lovely Supanna Matcha, Hanuman is able to complete the causeway within the prescribed time. Sukreep hurries to inform Phra Ram that the work is done, and the king's joy soars to the sixteenth heaven.

The army of monkeys, with fur neatly combed and polished, with accoutrements correctly slung and gleamingly furbished, its banners hoisted and snapping in the breeze, is marched to the beginning of the causeway and drawn up in order. Phra Ram mounts his victory chariot and reviews his troops. Looking on their serried ranks with pride, he delivers his order of the day. "Now the real battle against the demons begins. Soldiers, do your duty!"

The monkeys then file out along the causeway and onto Longka island, cheering as Phra Ram rides slowly across to enemy territory. The air resounds with martial music, and unseen angels release a gentle rain of flowers.

In this auspicious way, the seige of Longka begins.

92. *Hanuman makes love to Supanna Matcha*

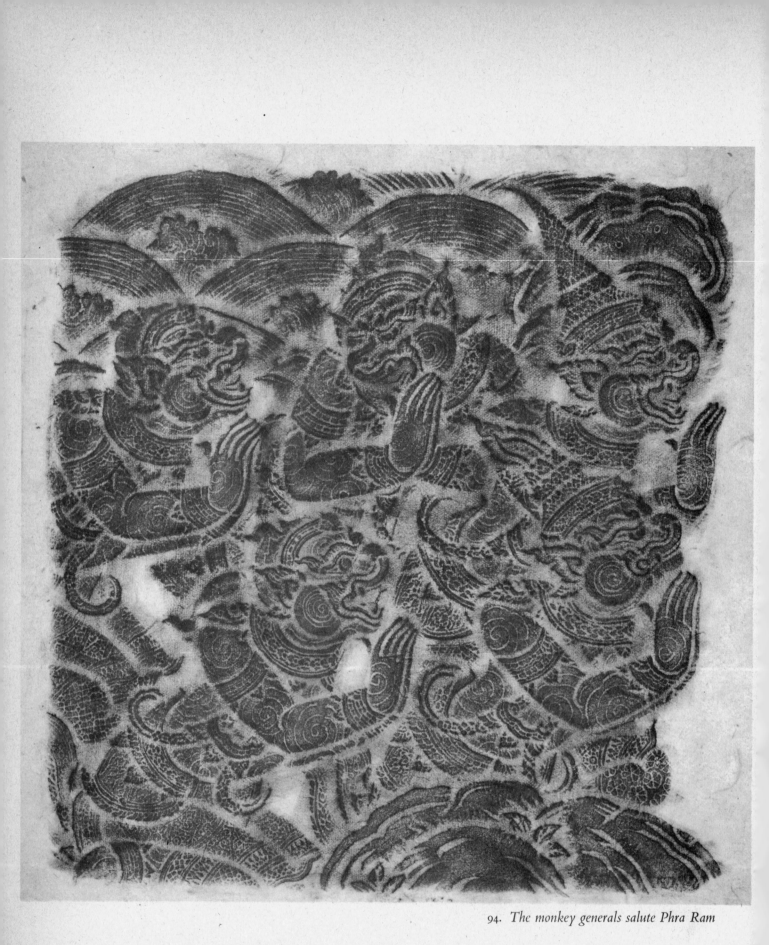

94. *The monkey generals salute Phra Ram*

93. *Phra Ram rides over the causeway to Longka*

95. *Prakontan leads Hanuman to the enchanted plain*

Totsagan, king of the demon city of Longka, has been following the progress of the monkey army closely. When he realizes that the invasion of his island is close at hand, he summons the giant Panurat and instructs him to bring about the speedy end of the invader. He tells Panurat to hide himself beneath the surface of the small and barren plain that lies not far from the end of the causeway, allowing only his hair to show above the soil. Using his demoniacal gifts, Panurat is to transform the plain into a park, a turfy place through which the breezes blow and the streams flow abundantly. Each of his hairs is to be changed into a flowering plant, a blossom-covered bush or a fruit-laden tree, and the air is to be filled with an irresistible fragrance. If this is done, says Totsagan, the monkeys are certain to make the place their camp. Then, as soon as they have settled in, Panurat is to rise out of the ground, blasting the place with his foul breath and picking the men and monkeys from his hair, to be crushed like lice. For the successful accomplishment of this task, Totsagan promises Panurat half his kingdom. The giant bows low before the king, assures him of his certainty of success, and hurries away to the plain.

One of Phra Ram's first acts on reaching the Longka end of the causeway is to send out the spirit Prakontan to search for a suitable campsite. The scout quickly returns with the news that he has found the perfect site quite close at hand. He describes the flowers, the water and the trees, and soothsayer Pipeck, who knows Longka as his home, is deeply puzzled. He can remember no park in the place described by Prakontan, and says as much to Phra Ram. On his advice, Hanuman is sent out with the spirit to reconnoiter the site.

96. *Hanuman discovers the giant Panurat*

On reaching the enchanted plain, Hanuman snuffs the scented air and looks about him with darting eyes that miss no detail.

"Congratulations," he says, "an excellent site, Prakontan. I couldn't have found a better myself. Firm, turfy ground, abundant flowing water, and plenty of wholesome fruit, which is just what we monkeys live on. Why, the place might have been laid out exactly for our convenience." But even as he speaks, he notices that there are no spoor near the streams, no birds sing among the blossoms, and not so much as a single ant is to be seen on the ripe fruit hanging from the boughs.

"Too good to be true," says Hanuman to himself and without further ado dives head first into the ground to see what lies at the bottom of the business.

95. *Prakontan leads Hanuman to the enchanted plain*

96. *Hanuman discovers the giant Panurat*

He immediately finds himself face to face with a very surprised giant. "And who are you, old earthworm?" he demands, flourishing his sword. "Answer, or eat the dust!"

Panurat gives a frightful roar, springs out of his hiding place and snatches up his cudgel.

"Learn some manners through the thick end of my stick, ignorant monkey," he bellows and aims a deadly blow at Hanuman's head.

97. *Hanuman decapitates Panurat*

Within seconds the two are locked in combat, each breathing out the most lurid threats. But it takes more than a giant to match the skill and cunning of the Son of the Wind. He allows Panurat a couple of passes to see what kind of foe he is dealing with, and then with a dazzling piece of swordplay, brings the giant helpless to his knees, and hacks off his head.

Looking around him, Hanuman sees that the "park" has reverted to its original barren and waterless state.

98. *Hanuman brings Panurat's head to Phra Ram*
99. *Phra Ram praises Hanuman*

When Phra Ram is informed of Hanuman's exploit and sees the head of the demon, he has high praise for the Son of the Wind. Prakontan, however, whose injudicious choice would have placed the whole army in the gravest danger, is ignominiously dismissed.

On the advice of the wise Pipeck, a camp is established in the Marakot Hills. At a council of war held there when the army has settled in, it is decided that Ongkot, the son of Palee and Nang Monto, shall be sent as envoy to Totsagan.

100. *Ongkot confronts Totsagan*

By this time even the appearance of a monkey is enough to cause consternation, if not strike terror, in the hearts of the demon citizens of Longka. So when Ongkot comes to the main gate of the city, the watchmen in the twin towers raise the alarm and the great doors are swung to and bolted against him. From the ramparts above the moat the demon rabble raises up a clamor of curses, cries and imprecations so deafening that the very kites wheel higher in alarm. Standing on the causeway across the moat, looking up at the crowded ramparts, his intelligent face registering contempt and disgust at the hullabaloo raised by the demons, Ongkot waits until he can be heard and then shouts up:

"I am the ambassador of the god Narai: my duty is to speak with your master, the ten-headed King Totsagan." But this speech is wasted, for the demons either fail to understand him of refuse to believe his words, and neither deliver his message nor open the gates.

99. *Phra Ram praises Hanuman*

98. *Hanuman brings Panurat's head to Phra Ram*

Ongkot waits until his patience is exhausted. Then he murmurs a spell to himself. Immediately, his body begins to grow and continues until he is so huge that he can blot out the light of the sun with his hands. A premature twilight settles over Longka. The birds go to roost and the bats sally forth from their eaves.

Interrupted in his affairs of state by this phenomenon, Totsagan sends to learn the reason for the darkness. The reply comes that the cause is a monkey colossus named Ongkot who demands to speak to him. At the word Ongkot, the darkness strikes through to the king's soul. This is the monkey, born of his own wife Monto, who has already brought him misery, humiliation and loss. With a sense of deep foreboding, he orders that the envoy be admitted and instructs his wife to prepare a banquet worthy of one who is the ambassador of Phra Narai.

The beautiful Nang Monto obeys him, her heart sad with the certainty that this meeting must end badly for either her husband or her son.

Totsagan's courtesies to the envoy have come too late, however. Incensed beyond endurance at the delay and enraged by the taunts of the demons on the walls, the hot-tempered Ongkot throws patience and protocol to the wind and breaks in the main door. Striking aside the guard and putting the demon citizens to flight before him, the masterful monkey strides through the streets until he comes to the palace. Without waiting to be announced he stalks through the apartments until he comes to the audience chamber, where Totsagan is still preparing to receive him.

Without ceremony, without salutation, the angry monkey strides to the throne. Seeing that no stool has been brought for him, he enlarges his tail, coils it beneath him, and thus raised to the level of the enthroned king, sits himself upon it.

Surprised and angry, and yet restraining his emotions, Totsagan gently reprimands the ambassador.

"How is it that you neglect the courtesies customary when dealing with a king?" he asks. "Speak, my good monkey."

"Monkey I am indeed, O king, but of a royal and divine line," Ongkot replies. "This being so, it is I who should complain of courtesies denied. But rather then waste words, I take action to raise myself to the level of a king, as is my right." And before Totsagan can reply to this rude speech, Ongkot produces a palm leaf, on which the terms of his mission are set forth, and from it reads Phra Narai's message:

"The Great Discus Maha Jakri, the Lord of the Bird Krut, the King and God, sends his Ambassador the Prince Ongkot to Totsagan, the King of the Demons. The subject of this embassy is the divine Lady Lakshmi, whom the great and powerful Lord Totsagan did seize from her master and wrongfully abduct to his kingdom beyond the ocean. Lord Totsagan is required to return this lady to the feet of her master, the divine king, Phra Ram Jakri."

Hearing this, Totsagan grinds his teeth. "How am I to understand this?" he shouts. "Who here is accused of abduction?   Look about this court and ask here who needs to steal, abduct or otherwise wrongfully acquire a wife."   At the thought of Nang Seeda and all that she means to him, Totsagan's self-possession deserts him. With mounting anger, he leans from his dais to glare at Ongkot.   "What is it you mean, monkey? Or perhaps it is more apposite to demand what it is you are doing at this court with your silly tale.   There was a happy time not long ago when there were so few of your kind that one could pass from one end of the kingdom to the other without so much as seeing a monkey.   Now it seems that the whole world teems with vermin. Even here to my court they come—first the insolent Hanuman, and now, even worse, a ruffian of your sort."

"Release the lady and 'vermin' will no longer trouble you," says Ongkot, his temper rising again at the sting of the insults.

"Never!" says Totsagan decisively, "I found the lady weeping and unprotected in the wild forest.   Out of charity I extended to her my protection and I shall continue to hold her by right."

"So be it," says Ongkot.   "Your stubbornness means the end of the demons. We have already rid the world of a number of your brothers, and soon, with the power vested in us by the gods, we shall complete the business."

At the reminder of these recent losses, Totsagan's faces darken.   "Yes. Out in the forest you were able to murder my brothers," he says.   "But the taking of a fortified and defended city is altogether another matter. Before Longka's armies, the two little men, your masters—and their monkey rabble—will be put to flight like spray before the wind."

"So you say," counters Ongkot.   "But you would be wiser to remember that Phra Ram and Phra Lak are born on earth expressly to kill you and the whole demon brood."

"A child's tale, and you believe it," Totsagan taunts the envoy.   "Demons defeated by lesser breeds like the monkeys. Do you hear this?"   Totsagan turns to the demons about the chamber with a sneer so that the entire assembly bursts into mocking laughter, and the chamber rings with the harsh sound.

Almost blind with rage, Ongkot allows the laughter to die down.   Then in a quiet, controlled voice, and yet with a clarity that carries to the furthest doors of the chamber, he says:

"Perhaps it was a dream I had when I was a youth—merely a dream that my father King Palee captured a giant crab that lay waiting in a stream to seize his son. Perhaps I only dreamed that the crab reassumed the form of a ten-headed king, and as such was given a merciless whipping and then allowed to drag himself back to Longka in shame.   But was it only my dream, great king, or did you share in it too? Is it possible that . . ."

But Totsagan can stand no more of this quiet voice that with every word lays open the scars across his back. Leaping to his feet, he screams, "Seize him!   Slit his throat!   Cut out his tongue!"

And the rest of the words are drowned by the shout of the demons as they start forward to lay hold of the insolent envoy.

100. *Ongkot confronts Totsagan*

101. *Four guards try to seize Ongkot*

Four guards nearest the throne are the first to lay hands on Ongkot. By this time the envoy has reduced his tail to its normal size and is ready for whatever may happen. Seeing that he cannot hope to escape the court by the way he entered, Ongkot seizes the four guards and springs onto the roof of the palace. From there he throws the struggling demons to their death on the bone-shattering flags of the courtyard below.

102. *Ongkot breaks down the palace gate*

While the demons are mustering the courage to attack him, Ongkot decides he has time for a final affront to to the Longka court. He snaps off the ridge piece of the roof and the carving of the four-faced guardian god Prom and throws them down to break into pieces at Totsagan's feet.

Above the uproar Ongkot hears the demon king shout despairingly, "Will no one bring me the head of this monkey ambassador?" and knows that it is time for him to go. With a final taunt of "Yours is the head that will roll, not mine," Ongkot flies up into the air and, having thrust aside the two doormen and smashed the palace doors, returns to the monkey camp.

Heartbroken and filled with shame, the demon king retreats to his inmost sanctum. He has been insulted before his own court, four of his guards have been butchered before his eyes, the tutelary god of the palace has been cast down, and a pack of monkeys has invaded his kingdom and threatens to invest his capital.

Alone in his chamber, he broods on these reverses. How will it all end, he wonders.

103. *Totsagan's nephews ride to the underworld*

After a long night of thought, Totsagan sends for his two nephews Nonyawik and Waiyuwake. Having received their salutations, he tells them to arm and prepare themselves for a long journey. They are to ride to the underworld to deliver a message to the lord of that realm, the giant Maiyarap, requesting him to come to the aid of Longka.

104. *Maiyarap, Lord of the Underworld, receives Totsagan's nephews*

The two men ride until they come to Badan, where Maiyarap has his kingdom, and are passed through the many gates and guards that surround the palace, until they are brought into the giant's presence. Prostrating themselves before him, Nonyawik and Waiyuwake deliver Totsagan's greetings and read his embassy.

Maiyarap is greatly upset to hear of the trouble his ally has been having and complains only that the request for aid has not come sooner. Having seen that the envoys have refreshed themselves, he sends them back to Totsagan with the assurance that he himself will lead his army to the relief of Longka with all speed.

101. *Four guards try to seize Ongot*

102. *Ongkot breaks down the palace gate*

103. *Totsagan's nephews ride to the underworld*

104. *Maiyarap, Lord of the Underworld, receives Totsagan's nephews*

105. *Maiyarap smashes his chariot*

When Maiyarap's mother—a woman of great wisdom and sound judgement—hears of her son's preparations to raise an army and march to Longka, she hurries to see him. She tells Maiyarap that Phra Ram has come to earth to overthrow the demons and predicts that he will be involved in their destruction if he throws in his lot with Totsagan. She advises him strongly to remain in Badan and let matters above take their course, pleads with him when he continues with his preparations for the campaign, and finally warns him that she will withhold her blessing if he rejects her advice.

Maiyarap, at the best of times subject to an uncertain temper, now falls into a violent rage at this opposition to his will. The courtiers withdraw and servants flee when they see their master in this dangerous condition, for in his rages Maiyarap has been known to destroy even what is dear to him. Now, shouting and cursing, the giant strides through the palace while his mother weeps, and in an extremity of passion takes his fine chariot by the shafts and dashes it to the ground, at the same time killing the draught lions. This act of wantonness partly assuages his rage, and Maiyarap proceeds with the mustering of his army and without further delay marches it to Longka.

106. *Maiyarap conducts magic rites*

Totsagan greets the Lord of the Underworld warmly. Having seen that his men are comfortably quartered, he prepares a sumptuous banquet for Maiyarap. In the course of this banquet, when the wine has been flowing freely, the hotheaded Maiyarap expresses his determination to take the field against Phra Ram immediately, and it is only by using all his guile that Totsagan is able to persuade him that a far better and surer method of bringing about the downfall of their enemy is not by frontal assault, but through the use of the magic powers with which Maiyarap is richly endowed. The Lord of the Underworld, who thirsts after the glories of victory in the open field, reluctantly agrees to return to Badan to prepare himself for occult rather than overt exploits.

Some days later, Maiyarap retires to a shrine in a secluded part of his kingdom and there, clad in sacred robes, seated before a fire over which an iron cauldron is hung, he joins his hands and sinks into a trance. Even as his mind is retiring from the world of everyday things to the shadowy realm of insubstantiality, his lips mutter ancient incantations, and the preparation in the cauldron begins to undergo a transformation. It is Maiyarap's intention to create a magic dust, for he knows that if his ceremony is carried through to its conclusion the preparation will have such strength that no being, whether of the earth, the heaven or the underworld, will be able to withstand him.

The gods, however, have so disposed things that those who can win the greatest powers are those who will use them best. Maiyarap's life has been far from austere, and it is a natural consequence that his trance is as

105. *Maiyarap smashes his chariot*

106. *Maiyarap conducts magic rites*

troubled and shallow as the sleep of a man who has eaten too well. Impressions, shapes, wraiths begin to stream into his disordered mind, and he is unable to dismiss them. They become clearer and more definite the longer he meditates, until at last they can leave him and take on a life of their own.

First to appear in the shrine are two women of pleasure who dance lewdly before his eyes. Maiyarap starts up furiously and destroys them, but his concentration has been broken, and he must return to the iron cauldron and begin once more the slow process of muttering incantations while sinking back into his trance.

But now two elephants appear and lock in furious combat, filling the shrine with the dust and shrill trumpeting of their battle. And once more Maiyarap has to break off his ceremonies to dismiss these creatures with his hollow wand before he can return again to the realm of insubstantiality.

When on the third attempt two lions appear and fight savagely before him, Maiyarap realizes that the performance of the complete ceremony is beyond him, so he seizes the beasts, tears their hearts from their bodies, and adds these potent organs to the material already in the cauldron, hoping that the dust thus constituted will be sufficiently powerful to bring about the downfall of Phra Ram and his army. He then returns to his city, Badan.

There he has an ominous dream. His court astrologer interprets it as a warning that if he goes to Longka, Waiyawik, the son of his sister Pirakuan, will become the lord of the underworld in his place. To forestall this, Maiyarap has Waiyawik and Pirakuan placed under heavy guard. Satisfied that the danger is thus averted, the rash Maiyarap returns to Longka, taking with him the magic dust.

107. *Maiyarap enters the sleeping Hanuman's mouth*

Phra Ram also has a dream of ill omen. The wise Pipeck correctly interprets it as a forewarning that an attempt will be made in the coming night to steal the king away from his army and warns that the only way to avert this danger is by keeping a strict watch until dawn the next day. Hearing this, Hanuman decides that he will play a part in the protection of Phra Ram. That evening he recites a spell that makes him grow to the size of a fortress. Thus enlarged, the Son of the Wind opens his mouth and places Phra Ram, Phra Lak and Pipeck inside. With his tongue as the door, Sukreep as the doorman and the eighteen royal generals as watchmen, Hanuman feels sure that his master will be safe. He curls his tail, which is the size of a great town wall, around the entire camp and, with his eyes wide open and his mind on the alert, he waits for the morning.

Maiyarap has been observing these precautions from close at hand, and overhears the order, "No monkey is to sleep until dawn!" Amused at the simplicity of his foes, the Lord of the Underworld flies high into the heavens and in the east suspends his magic diamond Gomin. This gem is so bright that the monkeys mistake it for the morning star and, thinking that dawn is at hand, believe the time of danger is past. Worn out by their vigil, many of them curl up on the ground where they are and fall asleep. Others, stretching and

yawning, leave their posts and go off in search of comfortable bowers in which to catch up on their rest. Even Hanuman closes his eyes and sinks into a light sleep.

Satisfied that no one is watching, Maiyarap flies over the camp and scatters the magic dust onto the monkeys, deepening their slumber. Then he leaps into Hanuman's mouth, steps over the recumbent bodies of Phra Lak and Pipeck, picks up Phra Ram, and makes off with him.

108. *Maiyarap flies to the underworld with Phra Ram*

Swiftly Maiyarap flies back to Badan, where he places the sleeping Phra Ram in an iron cage. He ensures that his nephew Waiyawik is still safely locked away, and orders his sister Pirakuan to set to work drawing water from the magic lake outside the walls of his palace, intending that on the morrow Phra Ram and Waiyawik should be boiled alive.

109. *Hanuman fights with Matchanu*

When the monkeys find that Phra Ram has vanished, Pipeck is able to tell them what has happened to him. Hanuman is chosen to recover the lost leader, and having prostrated himself at the feet of Phra Lak he sets off for the underworld, following the directions the seer has given him.

The way is not easy. The path soon comes to an end at a lotus pool. In the middle of this pool, severed from its stalk and floating on the green surface, is a particularly lovely lotus flower. Puzzled, Hanuman bounds this way and that, looking for a possible entrance to the underworld. Suddenly, the answer comes to him—the lotus stalk. He examines the end of the stalk closely, and there, sure enough, is a tiny passageway. Having recited a spell that causes his body to shrink, he squeezes into this passageway and shoots down it until he falls out into a completely different world, right in front of the outer walls of the city of Badan.

A thousand demons stand watch along the walls, but Hanuman does not permit them to detain him long. Grasping his trident firmly, he leaps among them, striking left, right and center, using his weapon to such effect that within a few minutes there is not a live demon watchman in all Badan. As he pushes on into the city, however, a huge and furious elephant charges him. Hanuman vaults lightly onto its neck and stabs it to death. Next he comes to a line of flaming volcanoes. He flies to a peak and there stamps about so heavily that the mountains collapse, extinguishing the flames. Next, swarms of mosquitoes, each the size of a partridge, attack him and try to drain him of his blood. Hanuman coolly crushes them as they fly at him until not one remains.

In the very center of the city he comes to a second lotus pool. By this time his hostile reception in the underworld has slightly ruffled his normal good humor, so that when a strange figure—half-monkey and half-fish—pops up on the surface of the pool and shouts at him rudely, "Now then, what are your doing here? Be off quickly, before I lay my hands on you." his irritation is such that his first impulse is to deal with it as he has

108. *Maiyarap flies to the underworld with Phra Ram*

dealt with Badan's other guardians. Noticing that the little figure is really remarkably handsome, however, despite the fish tail, he masters his irritation and calls out: "Well spoken, small fry! Now be a good lad and show me the way on from here."

This impertinence so infuriates the guardian of the pond that instead of answering, he snatches up a lotus flower and fetches the Son of the Wind a resounding blow across the head with it.

"That's the last time I try to be polite to a watchman," says Hanuman, and launches himself at the little beast, meaning to crush the life out of it. To his astonishment he finds the creature well able to take care of itself, and he receives quite as good as he gives in the ensuing conflict. After a furious struggle, they both draw back and look at each other with a new respect. When Hanuman has recovered his breath, he tries a fresh tack.

"Look here, young fellow," he says, "what are you doing down here? You are at least half a monkey, and yet you are working for the demons, our deadly enemies. Who are you, and how did you come down here? Speak up now, and tell me all about yourself."

"Well," says the little one, "the fact is I'm called Matchanu. My mother is the Queen of the Sea, Supanna Matcha, and my father is Maiyarap, King of the Underworld. That is, my foster father is Maiyarap. My mother, you see, is Totsagan's daughter, and when she found that she was going to give birth to me, she was terrified—not being married—as to what her father would say. As soon as I was born, she decided to leave me to whatever fortune the gods thought suitable for a foundling. I can't say I blame her. Totsagan is supposed to have a very nasty temper when he's crossed. Well, to cut a long story short, Maiyarap found me and, not having a son of his own, decided to adopt me. He brought me back here from the overworld, and set me up as guardian of this pond. I must say I'm grateful to the old boy, because its more than my real father, Hanuman, ever did for me."

When the Son of the Wind hears this, his heart almost bursts with paternal pride. "Well, bless me," he says, slapping his thigh, "I might have known it. Handy with your fists, hot-tempered and handsome—in other words, a real chip off the old block. My boy, prepare yourself for a surprise. You are now looking at your true father, Hanuman the Brave, no less." He preens himself.

But Matchanu hoots with laughter. "A likely tale," he says. "My father is a bit out of the ordinary. Supanna Matcha told me that I would know him because he can exhale the sun and moon from his mouth. If you can do that, my dear sir, I'm prepared to believe your claim, but otherwise…"

No sooner are these words out of his mouth than Hanuman has leapt into the air and breathed sun, moon and stars into the wondering sky. Matchanu immediately throws himself dutifully on his knees. "Please accept my apologies, father," he says. "I really didn't know…"

"Not at all," says Hanuman, "you were quite right to stop me. But you should know that I'm trying to find Phra Narai, and I need to be directed to Maiyarap's castle."

109. *Hanuman fights with Matchanu*

181

Now this places Matchanu in an invidious position. Gratitude to Maiyarap requires him to remain silent, yet filial devotion urges him to give an answer. He compromises by giving the direction in the form of a riddle.

"Not in the air, nor on the ground,
But through the water you must go—
Completely dry. For it is so
That what is lost may yet be found."

The Son of the Wind understands immediately. He thanks his son and, having caused his body to shrink again, once more enters a tiny passageway in a lotus stalk at the center of the pool and follows it down into the heart of Maiyarap's kingdom.

110. *Pirakuan's weight breaks the scales*

This time the passageway ends beside a large lake at the front of a splendid castle. While Hanuman is studying the layout of the place and wondering where Phra Ram might be, the main gate opens, and out comes the unhappy Pirakuan. Hanuman hides himself, and as Pirakuan fills her jars at the lake, the Son of the Wind hears her sigh heavily and say to herself, "Alas, that a mother should have to draw water to be used to boil alive her own son. And what evil destiny requires me to play a part in destroying the noble Phra Ram?"

At this, Hanuman immediately presents himself to Pirakuan and quickly convinces her that the only hope of saving her son lies in smuggling him into the castle. To do this Hanuman shrinks himself to the size of a lotus fiber and hides himself in the seam of Pirakuan's dress.

When Pirakuan returns to the castle gate, the demon watchmen weigh her, as they do everybody entering and leaving the castle, thus saving themselves the task of searching for contraband and hidden weapons. Pirakuan has been in and out of the gates innumerable times, so they know her weight to a hair. On this occasion, however, instead of balancing exactly, the scales give a mighty groan and break into pieces. Hanuman is to blame, of course, for although he has changed his size, he did not think to change his weight.

The watchmen are furious. How are they going to explain this to their officer, they ask themselves, and where are they to get another pair of scales? "We're going to kill you for this," they shout at Pirakuan. "Just wait while we think of a particularly fiendish way of doing it." At Hanuman's prompting, Pirakuan says, "Well, what do you expect of a pair of scales that has been used for the last one hundred thousand years?" adding, with a sigh, "Anyway, life is so terrible that I'd just as soon die now as later. At least I'll have the satisfaction of knowing that you will have to draw the water yourselves instead of idling away your time beside this gate." This gives the demons something to think about, and they talk the business over among

themselves, agreeing that they should not act too hastily. The upshot of the matter is that they let Pirakuan pass on into the castle, contenting themselves with uttering threats of future punishment.

Once inside, Hanuman reverts to his normal size. Pirakuan leads him to an inner garden where Maiyarap is sleeping in the shade—it is midafternoon by underworld reckoning and very warm—and having led him to the cage where Phra Ram is imprisoned, leaves him to deal with the matter as he thinks fit.

Ten million soldiers lie snoring about the cage. Hanuman's bright eyes dance with glee when he thinks what a fine fight they will provide him with, but he restrains himself. "Later, valiant monkey," he says to himself and turns to the business of releasing Phra Ram. It does not take him long. With one spell he deepens the sleep of the soldiers and with another he makes the iron bars of the cage bend back with a groan to admit him. He picks up the still sleeping Phra Ram tenderly, hurries back with him to the upper world and there places him at the summit of a mountain. "Angels, watch over him while I'm gone," he shouts into the heavens, "or there'll be the devil to pay!"

Then quickly he returns to the underworld.

III. Hanuman fights Maiyarap

Reaching the part of the park where the Lord of the Underworld lies stretched out asleep, Hanuman strikes a pose and sings out, "Awake, O unrighteous king. Know that Hanuman the Mighty, Hanuman the Brave is ready to slay you. The Lord of Death stands at your door and demands admittance." Lying on his couch, however, Maiyarap is in such a deep sleep that he does not hear this pretty speech, and Hanuman has to give him a kick to wake him. Immediately Maiyarap springs up with a snarl and lashes out with his sword at the intruder.

The Son of the Wind coolly ducks the blow, snatches the sword out of Maiyarap's hand and snaps it in two. Maiyarap now picks up a club and swings at him with it, but Hanuman smashes it to fragments. Maiyarap tries a spear, but the monkey shivers it to a thousand pieces, and the Lord of the Underworld is reduced to fighting with his bare hands. At the point of Hanuman's blade he is forced back into a corner of the garden, where he suddenly seizes a palm tree and lashes the Son of the Wind three times across the head with it. He might have been using a blade of grass for all the effect it has. In his turn, Hanuman takes up a palm trunk and strikes out at Maiyarap, bringing him to his knees. The Lord of the Underworld is quickly up again, however, and fights back as if unaffected by the blows.

At this point, Pirakuan, who has been watching the fight anxiously, calls out to Hanuman, "If you want to kill my evil brother, you must first crush his soul, which lives in a palm tree as a bumblebee at the top of the Trikot Mountains." At this, Maiyarap cries out from pain and rage, while Hanuman, stretching himself beyond belief, reaches to the top of the Trikot Mountains and catches the bee.

"Funny kind of a soul," says Hanuman tauntingly to Maiyarap, crushing the bee to death before his eyes,

"I'm sure you won't miss it." And then he takes his sword and slits Maiyarap's throat from ear to ear. The battle is over.

Hanuman ascends the throne of the underworld. In a solemn ceremony and enjoying every moment of it, he has Pirakuan's son Waiyawik brought before him. He raises the youth to the throne, enjoining him to rule Badan and the underworld with wisdom and justice. His own son, the fish-tailed Matchanu, he appoints adviser to the crown.

---

112. *Hanuman returns with Phra Ram and the head of Maiyarap*

Hanuman returns to the upper world to find Phra Ram safe in the care of the angels. He takes the sleeping king in his arms and flies back to Longka and the monkey camp, the severed head of Maiyarap held in one foot.

When Phra Ram is brought back to consciousness, he can hardly believe the story that the Son of the Wind tells him. Pipeck and his own brother Lak, however, confirm that he has indeed been abducted, while as material evidence to back his remarkable (and, to tell the truth, slightly embellished) account of the recovery, Hanuman is able to show the head of Maiyarap.

No longer in doubt, Phra Ram promises Hanuman that he shall one day be joint ruler of Ayutaya, giving him his ring in earnest of this reward. Hanuman throws himself gratefully before the king in acknowledgement of this honor.

112. *Hanuman returns with Phra Ram and the head of Maiyarap*

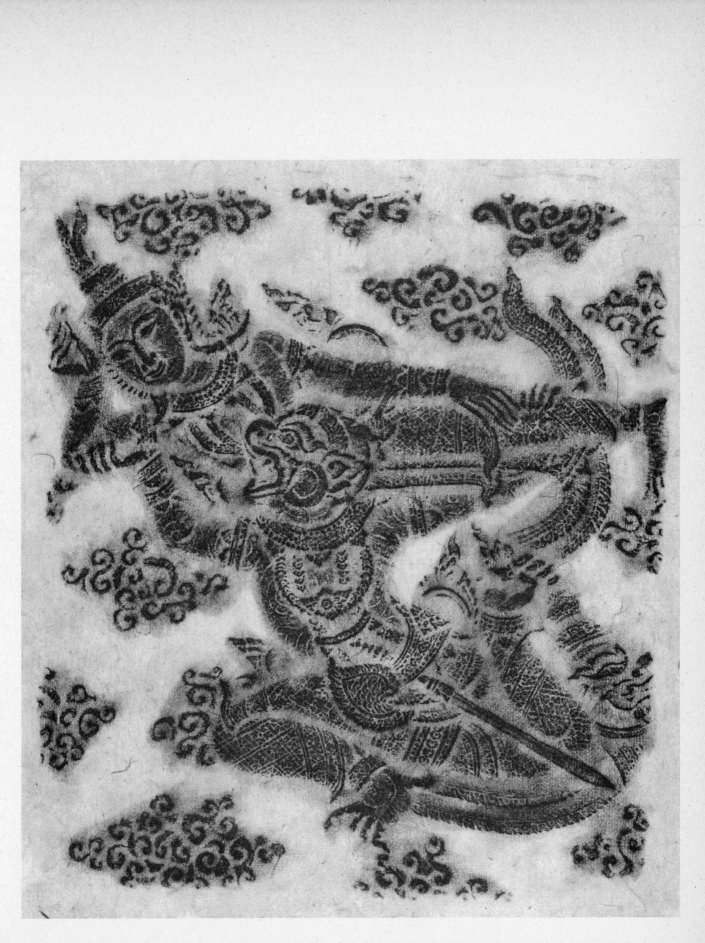

THE DEFEAT OF KUMPAGAN AND INTORACHIT

113. *Totsagan persuades Kumpagan to fight the monkey army*
114. *Demon courtiers attend Totsagan*

Totsagan is quickly informed of the death of his ally Maiyarap, and more than ever determined to defeat Phra Ram's army of monkeys, he sends for his younger brother Kumpagan, the Regent of Longka, the possessor of a magic spear. Kumpagan kneels before his brother and pays him due homage, but, on hearing that he has been chosen to take the field against Phra Ram, protests strongly.

"Brother," he says, "this war in which Longka is involved stems from your greed. If you had not stolen Nang Seeda from her lawful husband, there would now be no invaders on our soil. My advice is that you send Nang Seeda back to Phra Ram—and then we shall have peace again." The demon king bridles his anger at this outspokenness, knowing well how to deal with the honest but simple Kumpagan.

"My brother speaks as if he had no loyalties to the crown," he says. "He also forgets the injuries done us by Ayutaya. Must I remind him of the maiming of our sister Samanaka,* of our brothers, sons and allies slain, of the insults received at the hands of Ram's envoys?" "Nevertheless," says Kumpagan stubbornly, "it is clear who is in the right in this affair, and who in the wrong." Now Totsagan smiles down on his brother. "Kumpagan," he says softly, "help get rid of these people and you shall rule Longka with me. Is it agreed?"

At this juncture, a very strange thing happens. On many occasions in the past when Kumpagan has tried to dissuade his powerful brother from a course of action he considered dishonorable, his body dwindled until he became the size of an ordinary human being. And now, to his shame and horror, he once more finds himself shrinking before the baleful might of Totsagan.

Seeing this, the demon king gives a scornful laugh that rings over the entire court. "Why, look at my puny brother," he shouts. "Is this one of the race of giants, or does he perhaps belong to the monkeys and little people?"

At this, Kumpagan springs to his feet, unable to endure the public shame of his situation.

"Very well," he says furiously, "I'll fight, but no good will come of it." Even as he makes the resolution, his body begins to fill out, and within a moment he has regained his former size.

Gratified at his success, Totsagan commends his brother and advises him to prepare for battle with all speed.

---

* Incidents too numerous to relate in this narrative occur before the royal exiles reach the hermitage on the Kotawaree River. In one of them, Samanaka attempts to seduce Ram and Lak, and, when they spurn her, she attacks Nang Seeda. The brothers punish her by cutting off her lips, nose and ears, and thus mutilated, she returns to Longka where she persuades her brother Totsagan to take revenge on Ram by stealing his wife.

Before the battle begins, the demon seer Pipeck rides out to parley with his brother. His attempt to win Kumpagan over is ridiculed, however, and Pipeck is sent back to Phra Ram with the following riddle:

"A foolish monk*, a woman sly,

A tusker and a turncoat vile;

Just name these four—and naming, smile,

And we in war shall never vie."

Phra Ram declines to solve the riddle, and it is Ongkot who reveals that the monk is Phra Ram, the woman Samanaka, Totsagan's sister, the elephant Totsagan and the turncoat Pipeck—and that unless the royal brothers are prepared to concede the justice of these appellations, war is inevitable.

A whole series of battles follows this exchange. In the first, Kumpagan tricks Sukreep into a trial of strength. When the guileless commander in chief has exhausted himself, Kumpagan takes him prisoner, and only Hanuman is able to save him as he is being dragged—more dead than alive—from the field.

Following this, Kumpagan retires to a secluded place to endow his spear with even greater potency than it already possesses. Hanuman and Ongkot save the situation by transforming themselves respectively into a decomposing dog floating down a river and a vulture perched on and feeding from the stinking corpse, causing the demon to break off his ceremonies in disgust before they are complete. Kumpagan returns to the battlefield, and the two forces once more engage each other.

This time, Kumpagan succeeds in wounding Phra Lak with his magic spear, and for a time it seems that the wound must prove mortal. But once again the Son of the Wind saves the situation by flying to a distant mountain and there, with great difficulty, collecting herbs that heal Phra Lak completely.

Now the demon hits on a likely scheme. He finds the source of the stream supplying the monkey camp with water, turns himself into a dam across it, and prepares to remain in that position until the monkeys either die of thirst or call off their campaign. This time Hanuman transforms himself into a demon maiden and joins a party of the pleasure girls of the Longka court as they go out to amuse Kumpagan during his long and boring wait. Having found the demon, Hanuman quickly provokes him to a fight, and the waters are consequently released. The fight is inconclusive, but the demon has failed in his final stratagem and is brought to his last battle.

---

* It is not entirely clear why Phra Ram should be referred to as a monk, though during his stay at the hermitage by the Kotawaree River, he observed certain abstinences that perhaps entitle him to this appellation. He is foolish, of course, for having failed to protect Nang Seeda adequately.

114. *Demon courtiers attend Totsagan*

113. *Totsagan persuades Kumpagan to fight the monkey army*

116. *Two demon generals accompany Kumpagan*

115. *Kumpagan rides out to do battle*

117. Ongkot fights the demons of Kumpagan's army

118. Hanuman grapples with Kumpagan's demon generals

Pipeck casts Kumpagan's horoscope on the morning of the battle and, predicting that it will be his last day on earth, advises Phra Ram himself to take the field against the demon. Happy to lead his fine monkey army into battle at last, Phra Ram arms himself, prays to the gods for an auspicious outcome to the day and rides out at the head of his troops.

Kumpagan, on the other hand, takes the field after a wretched night and with a heavy heart. The kites swarm above his soldiers, their pennants droop spiritlessly, and the very weapons of the demon army seem to have lost their keenness.

From the first shock of contact, when the monkeys throw themselves valorously at the demon line, it is clear there can be only one outcome. Demons drop lifeless in such numbers that the chariots of either side are brought to a standstill, but even so the monkeys swarm eagerly forward, needing no urging from their commanders. Desperately hard pressed, Kumpagan shoots an arrow into the air, bringing down tongues of fire upon the monkeys. Phra Ram is quick to counter this by shooting his arrow Paladjan aloft, calling down torrents of rain sufficient not only to put out the fires but also to sweep away whole companies of demons, not to speak of horses, elephants and wagons. The Longka army, disheartened at these losses, gives ground, and Kumpagan has difficulty rallying his troops.

119. Kumpagan dies in Pipeck's arms

120. Phra Narai fires his arrow at Kumpagan

The leaders of the two armies now come face to face. Phra Ram unleashes his Akaniwat arrow at his adversary, and the lions drawing Kumpagan's chariot fall dead. The Regent of Longka fires his last arrow at Phra Ram as he comes to ride him down, but sees it hiss wide of the mark. With his great bow stave, Ram beats the demon to his knees and then draws back and fires the Promat arrow. Mortally wounded, crying out with a voice like the wind in the mountains, Kumpagan falls to the earth. His hands pluck at the arrow, but to no avail.

With his last breath, the Regent of Longka reconciles himself to his brother Pipeck and begs forgiveness of Phra Ram, whom he now recognizes to be the god Narai. Convinced that his contrition is sincere, Phra Ram commends the soul of the demon to the gods, and Kumpagan dies with the assurance that he will be received into paradise without delay.

In Longka, Totsagan quickly learns of the defeat of his younger brother and alone in his chamber mourns his death.

118. *Hanuman grapples with Kumpagan's demon generals*

120. *Phra Narai fires his arrow at Kumpagan*

119. *Kumpagan dies in Pipeck's arms*

Determined to turn the tide of the campaign in his favor, Totsakan calls on his mightiest general, none other than his own son by Nang Monto, Intorachit. Up to the present Intorachit has paid little attention to the war, but on being informed of the defeats and losses that Longka has sustained at the hands of Phra Ram, he throws himself on his knees before his father and begs permission to take the field against the invader immediately. Totsagan grants this request gladly.

Early in the morning, to the cheers of the citizens and the clamor of rumbling chariots and clashing arms, the demon army sallies forth from Longka, with Intorachit riding at its head. At the same time the monkey army, under the banner of the heavenly bird Krut and led by Phra Ram's royal brother Lak, marches out to oppose it. As the two hosts draw closer, Intorachit picks out his adversary and, having never seen a human being before, marvels at the fairness of skin and beauty of form of Phra Lak. Pitying him, he drives his chariot close to that of Phra Lak and calls to him, "You see before you Intorachit, the conqueror of the god In, the possessor of powers unequaled. In all the heavens I fear only the god Isuan. Take advantage of my clemency; disperse your army and leave the field, for nothing can withstand my magic arrows."

But Phra Lak calls out in reply:

"I am Phra Lak, brother of the god Narai. We have come to put down the insolent might of the demons. I too have power in my bow. Concede that Totsagan's life is forfeit and save your own."

While this parley is being conducted, the restless Hanuman has crept around to the rear of Intorachit's chariot and examined his weapons. Now he prances out in front of the demon and proceeds to mock his brave words.

"Who's afraid of those quills you're carrying, demon," he shouts. "Why, there's more might in this old trident of mine than in the combined weapons of your whole army. If you're so smart with a bow, give us a demonstration instead of talking so much." And he leaps up and down and somersaults and cartwheels and performs such antics in front of the demon army that Intorachit, insulted beyond endurance, selects an arrow, draws back his bow and lets fly at the Son of the Wind.

The arrows—the original shaft multiplying in flight—sigh like the wind in the trees as they fly and strike Hanuman with enormous force, bowling him head over heels in the dust. Although he is unharmed—for nothing can penetrate his diamond hide or in fact do him any damage at all—the sight of Hanuman laid low by the arrows enrages the monkeys, and they fall on their demon adversaries, slashing, hacking, scratching, biting, gouging and kicking, while the demons respond in their own fashion. The battle rages until nightfall, when both generals break off the conflict and retire to their camps. Many battles follow, none of which is decisive. Intorachit retires from the field, intending to perform rites that will heighten the power of his Nakabat arrow, and while he is absent a number of lesser generals prosecute the war, each succumbing in turn to the monkey army. Nevertheless, Intorachit gains some of the breathing space he requires. He invests his arrow with considerable power, and although one of his commanders—for reasons that will be related later—causes him to break off the ceremony before it is finished, Intorachit returns to the field sure that his shaft will be too strong for the enemy to resist. His confidence is well founded. When the armies are confronting each other once more and battle is about to be joined, Intorachit flies high into the air. Aiming at the monkey ranks, he lets fly his Nakabat arrow, and the air is filled with the hissing of innumerable snakes.

122. *Phra Ram's army is overcome by Intorachit's snake arrows*
123. *The bird Krut releases Phra Lak*
124. *Pipeck advises Ram to fire an arrow to summon the bird Krut*

The snake arrows—for this is the form in which the Nakabat shaft applies its power—fall like rain on the monkeys, binding their limbs and biting their bodies with venomous fangs. Even Phra Lak falls, and of all the army only Pipeck is left unscathed. Intorachit allows the demon to flee the field, glad that the news of this total defeat shall reach the ears of Phra Ram quickly. Triumphantly Intorachit marches his army back to Longka, savoring in advance the jubilant plaudits of the citizens and his father's immeasurable gratitude and pride.

This triumph, however, is premature. Pipeck has fled to Phra Ram not to inform him of his irreversible defeat, but to advise him how the situation may be remedied. Hurrying to the field of battle, Phra Ram fires his arrow Plaiwat into the air, summoning the bird Krut to his aid. That friend of the monkey army comes sighing down from the heavens and gets to work with flashing beak and ripping talons. In a trice, the snakes are torn loose and sent slithering down to the darkest corner of the underworld. As for the soldiers of Phra Ram's army, they are none the worse for their temporary setback. From Phra Lak, the eighteen royal generals and Hanuman, down to the humblest drummer monkey, they rise up, flex their stiff limbs, fall into their ranks and march back to camp in good order.

In Longka the royal demons, father and son, hear this news with fury. Together they discuss the situation, planning the next move in their campaign against Phra Ram.

125. *Phra Ram fires his Paladjan arrow*
126. *Wirunyamuk is caught in the diamond net*

Close as Intorachit came to defeating the monkey army in the battle of the snake arrows, he has reason to deplore the fact that but for a piece of bad luck his efforts would have been crowned with complete victory.

It happened like this. When the two armies had taken the field and the conflict had become general, Intorachit called on his ablest general, a demon with a good knowledge of the occult named Wirunyamuk, to

122. *Phra Ram's army is overcome by Intorachit's snake arrows*

121. *Intorachit fires his Nakabat arrow*

124. *Pipeck advises Phra Ram to fire an arrow to summon the bird Krut*

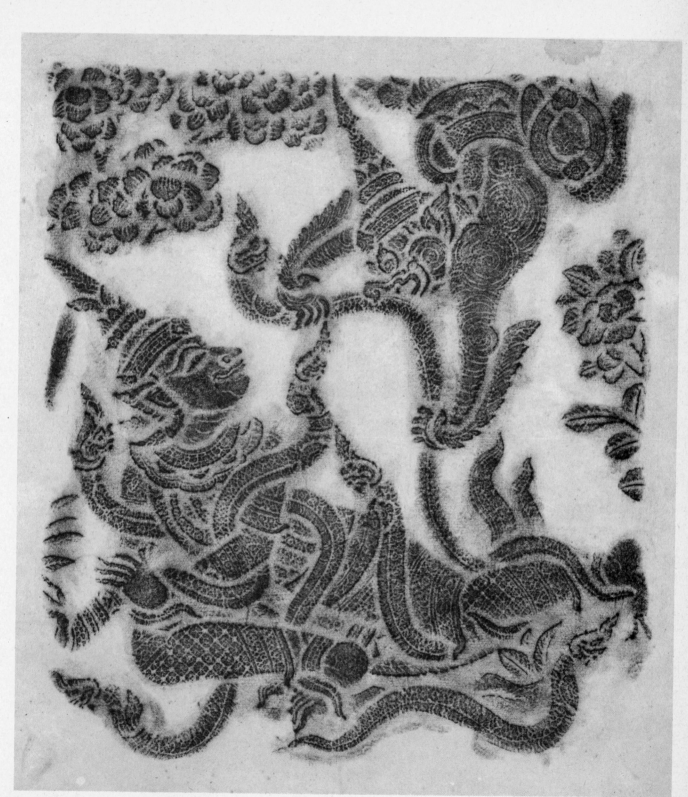

123. *The bird Krut releases Phra Lak*

126. *Wirunyamuk is caught in the diamond net*

125. *Phra Ram fires his Paladjan arrow*

take command of the army. He explained that although his Nakabat arrow already possessed great potency, he wished to retire for a short time to endow it with even greater power. Having told Wirunyamuk where he would conduct this ceremony and warned him that he was only to be disturbed in the case of the direst emergency, Intorachit put the command of the army into his hands and left the field.

He had not been gone long when the demons and giants became aware that their commander in chief had left them. Despite Wirunyamuk's entreaties and commands, despite even the threats of their generals, they lost their confident ferocity and began to give ground before the eager monkeys. To make a bad matter even worse, Wirunyamuk, with more valor than discretion, left the high ground from which he had been directing his troops and threw himself into the forefront of the battle. The monkeys were quick to grasp this opportunity, and under Ongkot's direction one wing of Ram's army cut Wirunyamuk from the main body of his force and called on him to surrender.

With his men around him going down before the swords of the monkeys, Wirunyamuk quickly recited a charm that made him invisible. The monkeys, suddenly deprived of their prize, let out a great howl of disappointment. Phra Ram, informed of what had happened, asked Pipeck what should be done, and the wise demon advised him to shoot his Paladjan arrow into the air.

Phra Ram drew back his bow and fired the arrow. As it flew above the place where Wirunyamuk had been fighting, it disappeared and was replaced by a net of diamond arrows. In the middle of the net, seated on the back of his great red-maned horse and struggling to free himself, was Wirunyamuk, no longer invisible. With one bound, Hanuman was on his back and having unhorsed him and deprived him of his weapons, he dragged the unfortunate demon to the feet of Phra Ram.

_____

127. *Wirunyamuk is trussed and beaten*

128. *Wirunyamuk is released by the monkeys*
_____

By this time the monkeys realized that Intorachit had left the field and, guessing that he was preparing mischief for them, demanded to know of Wirunyamuk where he had gone. The demon refused to tell them, so he was handed over to the monkey inquisition to be stripped, trussed and beaten without mercy. He still refused to say where Intorachit had gone, and this honorable silence was maintained when the monkeys, resorting to grosser torture, hacked off his right hand. He would even have suffered the ultimate penalty had not Phra Ram stepped in and released him, explaining that his death could not benefit them. And so a mark of infamy was tattooed on Wirunyamuk's forehead, and much to the monkeys' dissatisfaction, he was allowed to go free.

But this act of clemency brought its own reward. Wirunyamuk immediately flew to Intorachit, and rousing him from his deep meditation, told him that his army was leaderless and in danger of annihilation. Intor-

127. *Wirunyamuk is trussed and beaten*

128. *Wirunyamuk is released by the monkeys*

achit broke off the ceremony over his Nakabat arrow, trusting that its potency was already sufficient to bring about the downfall of the monkey army, and flew back to the battlefield.

The outcome of the snake arrow battle has already been related. Its inconclusiveness is now easy to understand.

129. *Hanuman, Ongkot and Sukreep attack Intorachit*

There comes a lull in the campaign.

No demon armies leave Longka's safe walls, and the monkeys camped near the city hear no sounds of preparation for further battle. Uneasy at this quiescence and suspecting that something is afoot, Phra Ram asks the seer Pipeck where Intorachit has gone and what he is doing.

From a deep trance, the seer speaks:

"Intorachit has left the city for seven days. In this time he intends to perform ceremonies to harden his body in magic fire. I see him now, seated on a meditation table of gold in a remote shrine. This shrine is located in a bamboo thicket on the slopes of Mount Jakrawan."

It is clear that unless these ceremonies are disrupted, Intorachit will become invincible, so Phra Ram orders his brother Lak to lead a shock party, composed of Hanuman, the eighteen royal generals and a body of troops, to attack the son of Totsagan.

Following the directions given them by the wise Pipeck, they quickly reach the slopes of Mount Jakrawan. Pushing carefully through the dense and airless bamboo thickets on the mountain's flank, they come on the shrine. Three circles of demons and giants guard it, their hideous aspect alone enough to frighten the wits out of anyone stumbling on the place by chance. Phra Lak disposes his men around the shrine and then fires an arrow at the building. With a noise like thunder the entire edifice collapses, scattering the demons, extinguishing the magic fire and waking Intorachit from his trance.

With a horrible shout, the monkeys put the guardian demons to flight, while bold Hanuman, with Ongkot and Sukreep supporting him, attacks the son of Totsagan, shouting as he does so:

"Well now, my demon princeling, what are you roasting yourself here for? Don't we make it hot enough for you on the battlefield? It really wasn't necessary for you to come so far, because we are going to burn Longka about your ears if you'll just wait a little."

130. *Phra Lak fires his Akaniwat arrow*
131. *Intorachit is hit by Phra Lak's arrow*

The furious Intorachit has snatched his mighty bow stave from the wall and attempts to smash his assailants, but he is so stiff from his long vigil that it is as much as he can do to get clear of the monkeys and scramble

129. *Hanuman, Ongkot and Sukreep attack Intorachit*

208

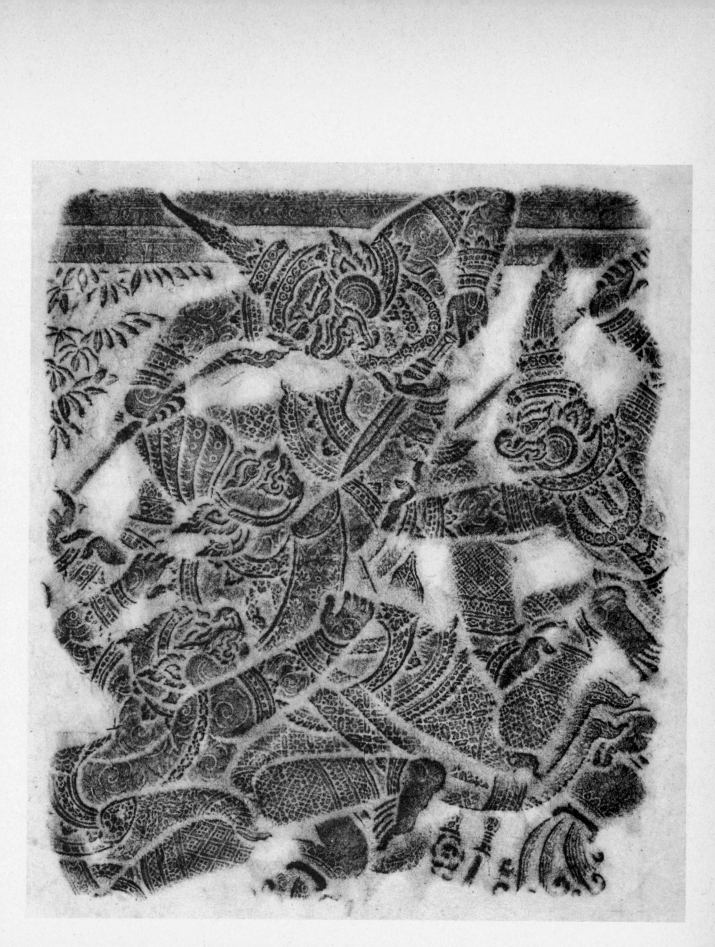

131. *Intorachit is hit by Phra Lak's arrow*

130. *Phra Lak fires his Akaniwat arrow*

aboard his lion chariot.   In it he swirls to a commanding position above the shock party, and prepares to make the monkeys and their human leader regret their temerity.   He selects his deadly Witsanu-Panam shaft, fits it to his bow and lets it loose.   It rushes down on the monkeys with a fearful roar, but Phra Lak quickly counters by firing his no less powerful Akaniwat arrow.   It hisses upwards, smashes the demon's arrow to fragments and then turning in flight, buries itself with tremendous force in Intorachit's breast.   Over goes the demon's chariot, and Intorachit, badly wounded, is thrown to earth.   Hidden by the thickets of bamboo, he has time to cut the shaft out of his wound and, while the hullaballoo of the monkey hunt draws nearer, decide quickly what he must do.

Severely weakened by his wound, and hardly less so by the privations of the last days, Intorachit realizes that neither the time nor the place of this fight are to his advantage.   Swearing that he will be revenged on his assailants at a later date, he hurls his discus into the air and, under cover of the violent storm that immediately breaks out, makes good his escape.

Well satisfied with the outcome of the expedition, Phra Lak calls together the elements of his troop and leads it back to the monkey camp.

---

132. *Nang Monto gives Intorachit her breast, while Totsagan looks on*

Utterly exhausted, Intorachit regains Longka city and reports to his father on this latest encounter with the invaders.

When Nang Monto sees the wound her son has sustained in his battle with Phra Lak her heart almost breaks. She takes her dearest child in her arms and gives him her breast, knowing that her milk will restore his full strength to him.   But even when he has recovered, she continues to hold him to her, stroking his head and crying, "Why should you suffer for the sins of your father, committed long before you were born?"   And while Intorachit is sleeping, dreaming of the battle he knows must be his last, Nang Monto rounds on the demon king and implores him to return Nang Seeda to Phra Ram, so that their son shall live.

But the poison of his desire for the wife of Ram taints even his love for Monto.

"You are speaking not for the love of your son, but out of jealousy of Seeda," he says viciously.   "And well may you be jealous, for I love her beyond all my possessions.   Be quite certain that if you keep your child from fighting tomorrow, I shall lead the army myself."

Intorachit, however, knows his duty.   When he has rested, he comes into the demon king's presence and, bowing low before him, begs to be allowed the honor of leading the demons against the invaders in the morning. Well pleased, Totsagan gives his permission and presents his son with the powerful arrow Sooragan to use against Phra Ram's army.

The demon prince leaves his father with a heavy heart.   Despite his brave words, he knows well what the outcome of the morning's battle will be.   He retires with his wife Suwanna Kanyuma for one last night of love.

132. *Nang Monto gives Intorachit her breast, while Totsagan looks on*

213

133. *Intorachit rides out to battle*

Early in the morning, when the sun is drawing up the mist from the battlefield, the demon army assembles before the walls of Longka. Before his residence, the resplendently accoutred Intorachit climbs into his chariot, and one by one, in their proper order, the members of the princely family—his wife Suwanna Kanyuma, his children, his concubines—pay their respects. His friends too, take their leave of him. After a final embrace and a fond word with his wife and a last backward glance at the palace in which he has spent so many happy hours, Intorachit drives swiftly along the main avenue, between cheering citizens, and out of the great gate of Longka.

Beyond the walls Intorachit takes his place at the head of his troops. After a few words of encouragement, he orders the advance.

The battle begins.

134. *Intorachit and Phra Lak come face to face*

As soon as he thinks an auspicious moment in the battle has been reached, Intorachit fires his father's arrow Sooragan at the enemy. Immediately, like leaves scattered before the wind, like stalks under the reaper's sickle, more monkeys fall than can be counted.

Seeing this, Phra Lak, the leader of the army of Ayutaya, fires his Promat arrow. It flies straight to Intorachit's chariot, bursting it asunder and throwing the demon to the ground. Giant and demon soldiers innumerable fall stricken to the earth, while the monkey casualties recover their senses and rise up ready to fight on.

Seeing that the tide of the battle is flowing against him, Intorachit savagely hews his way to Phra Lak's chariot and challenges the human prince to single combat. Hand to hand, using their great bows as staves, the two fight closely. Circling, striking mightily with their bows, each seeks an opening to land a telling blow. Backwards and forwards they range, the demons and monkeys calling a truce to watch this combat and ringing the princes in a wide circle. The sun himself swings higher, as if to seek a vantage point from which to view this unique trial of strength. Still they fight on, each with heaving chest and rasping throat, until, at the moment when it seems the combat will go on till nightfall, a blow from Phra Lak slips past Intorachit's guard and strikes the demon to his knees. In a flash, even as Phra Lak is aiming another blow at him, Intorachit mutters a magic spell that turns the stave aside as it falls. He then hurls his discus into the air, meaning to cut down the monkey army and his opponent, but Lak destroys it with his Promat arrow.

Now Intorachit is weaponless, and, surrounded by foes, sees defeat and death in every eye. With a final summoning of his powers, he calls up a violent storm, and springing up from the field of carnage, seeks refuge in the clouds.

133. *Intorachit rides out to battle*

134. *Intorachit and Phra Lak come face to face*

At a loss to know what to do next, Phra Lak consults his adviser Pipeck. The wise demon is able to see where Intorachit is hiding, and directs Phra Lak's aim, so that his Plaiwat arrow flies straight to the demon prince's breast, cloaked though he is in clouds. The shaft sinks home, and all Intorachit's efforts to loosen it are unavailing. Sobbing in agony as he tugs at the shaft and conscious that his strength is ebbing from him, the demon laments his coming death and the downfall of Longka.

From his chariot Phra Lak aims his Promat arrow, meaning to finish the demon. Pipeck quickly restrains him.

"Don't shoot, my lord," he calls. "The blood of Phra Prom flows in Intorachit's veins, and if so much as one drop falls to the ground, the earth will be consumed by fire. Let Ongkot fly to heaven to beg from Thada Prom the use of his diamond bowl. Both the head and blood of Intorachit can be caught in it, and no harm will be done."

So Ongkot is sent on his errand, and in no great time returns with the diamond vessel.

Now Phra Lak fires his Promat arrow at the expiring Intorachit. With a deafening roar it hurtles heavenward. It strikes Intorachit squarely, breaking his arms and severing his head from his body. Ongkot, waiting below the clouds, catches the head and blood, while the demon's body plunges to the earth in the vicinity of the Jakrawan Mountains. So ends the life of the mighty Intorachit, second in power only to Totsagan.

In the monkey camp, jubilation knows no bounds. Phra Ram embraces his brother on being told the good news and in an order of the day commends Phra Lak in the highest terms for his outstanding victory. Neither is the loyal Pipeck forgotten by his grateful lord.

In Longka, on the other hand, the blackest gloom prevails. When word of his son's death reaches him, shock and sorrow so strike Totsagan that he appears to age before the eyes of the messenger. As for Intorachit's mother and his wife Suwanna Kanyuma, their sorrow is inexpressible when they see the corpse of the prince borne into the city. For a time, Nang Seeda's life trembles in the balance, for Totsagan makes up his mind to execute her immediately by way of revenge and is only dissuaded with difficulty, his advisers urging that such an action can only bring immediate ruin to Longka. On reflection, Totsagan discovers that this advice is welcome, for despite the intense sorrow he feels at the loss of his son, his desire to possess Nang Seeda has not weakened.

Intorachit's cremation takes place amidst the rain and clouds of Mount Nilagala. As the flames consume his son's body, Totsagan finds his sorrow giving place to an even deeper hatred of the enemy. Looking at the grief-lined face of Nang Monto, whose tears for Intorachit flow without cease, Totsagan turns his mind afresh to plans for the defeat of Phra Ram's army.

Even before the end of the period of mourning for his son Intorachit, King Totsagan sends an envoy to his allies, Sahatsadecha the thousand-headed and his brother Mulplam, king and regent respectively of the country of Pangtan, asking their aid. The ambassador is well received and returns with the assurance that Pangtan will muster an army and march to Longka's relief with all speed. The first detachments, indeed, were already assembled and others were being formed when the envoy took his leave.

Totsagan is much heartened at this news. Banishing his personal sorrow, he commands the court and city of Longka to cast aside the appurtenances of mourning and defeat and put on the apparel of celebration. Soon bright flags float above the main avenue of the city, and beacons are lit along the palace walls, so that at night it appears that even the stars have allied themselves with Longka. When Sahatsadecha and his host arrive, the entire demon army is drawn up along the approaches to Longka and the citizens cram the walls and crowd the walks to add their tumultuous welcome to the reception of the ally. A great banquet is prepared that evening to set the royal seal on the occasion.

Totsagan has not stinted in his festal preparations. The very best of Longka's wines and foods are set out before the guests, who eat heartily and drink deep. Nor is there a shortage of entertainment, for jesters, conjurors and acrobats vie with each other for the attention of the lesser merrymakers, while the most graceful dancers and sweetest singers, the prettiest female demons in the whole kingdom demonstrate their classical arts before the royal table.

As one course succeeds another, and the empty flasks are replaced by full ones, the need for entertainment diminishes. Soon table competes with table, and soldier with soldier, in excesses of all kinds—of gluttony, horseplay, braggadocio and drunkenness. At the lowest end of the great hall, demon infantrymen dance on the tables and sing shrill love songs, while at the upper end the generals boast of their conquests and sink drunkenly to the floor.

While they share no part in the riots of their men, the royal brothers of Pangtan have also drunk well, and it needs no encouragement from Totsagan to keep them talking of the conduct of their recent campaigns and elaborating on the extent of their occult powers. Before long they are asking about the disposition and strength of Phra Ram's army and discussing how it might—no! more than might, can, indeed, will—be defeated. The discussion continues deep into the night, and much to Totsagan's satisfaction, his allies insist that they be allowed to lead their men against the invaders that very morning.

136. *Ongkot catches Intorachit's head in a diamond bowl*

135. *Phra Lak fires his Promat arrow at Intorachit*

137. *Totsagan gives a feast for Sahatsadecha and Mulplam*

138. *Classical dancers entertain the royal guests*

139. *Demon notables at their revels*

140. *Demon soldiers drink deep*

Before dawn the noise of the martial preparation within Longka comes to the ears of Phra Ram. Pipeck tells him that the new enemy is led by the royal brothers of Pangtan and advises that the monkey army should be commanded by Phra Ram himself, Phra Lak acting as his lieutenant.

The demon host that issues from Longka's gates shortly after the sunrise is even more monstrous in appearance than the ones that have preceded it. Mounted for the most part on horses and elephants, but with many another outlandish beast in evidence, it is led by Sahatsadecha, King of Pangtan. His figure unfailingly strikes terror into the heart of the most confident enemy. His body is enormous and supports one thousand terrible heads. From each of his one thousand mouths two fangs of white protrude, and as his other teeth are a green as grass, his rare smile is almost as much to be feared as his customary grimace. His two thousand arms each support a weapon, and these clash together as he advances with more noise than a complete army makes on the move. His chariot is enormous, partly because it has to bear his great weight but also because it must accommodate the many concubines without whom he never takes the field. Mulplam, his brother, is scarcely less terrifying in appearance, while Totsagan, King of Longka, who is accompanying his allies to the battlefield, is no sight for the timid, and all in all it may be said that the army pouring out of Longka on this occasion is as horrible as anything ever assembled in the Three Worlds.

No sooner has it cleared the city of Longka, however, than an odd and inauspicious event occurs. Out of nowhere a strong wind springs up, whirling columns of dust into the air and throwing down broken branches onto the demon ranks. The sky, which until this moment has been perfectly clear, is now covered with clouds so black and louring that the light is almost entirely blotted out. Peals of thunder reverberate between heaven and earth, and a sudden vivid bolt of lightning darts downward, striking and damaging Totsagan's chariot. No sooner has this happened than the storm passes, and the birds rise once more, singing in the clear and tranquil air. But Totsagan recognizes the mishap as an ill omen, and with the concurrence of his allies, returns to the city.

Eager to come to grips with the enemy, the demon brothers lead their army briskly on until they come to favorable ground not far from the monkey camp. There they dispose their forces for the coming battle, and wait confidently.

224

145. *Phra Ram and Phra Lak ride out to meet Sahatsadecha*

Word is quickly brought to Phra Ram that the demons have taken up their positions. The royal brothers mount their chariot, and, having assigned Ongkot to the rear guard, Hanuman to the van and Sukreep to the the main force of the army, they give the order to advance.

The monkeys march to the battlefield in high spirits and good order, but the moment they see the hideous Sahatsadecha at the head of his demons, they are so terror stricken that they turn tail with one accord and flee into a wood on their flank. Here they take to the trees, peering from the upper branches at the fearsome demon host, chattering and gibbering among themselves in the last extremity of terror. Of the entire army, only the royal brothers, commander in chief Sukreep, Hanuman, Ongkot, Chompooparn and the other royal generals stand their ground.

Sahatsadecha is astonished when he sees only this tiny band opposing him. He rides over to consult with his brother Mulplam, protesting that if he joins battle with this handful of humans and monkeys he will become— great warrior that he is—the laughing stock of the Three Worlds. Deciding that Totsagan has enormously exaggerated the monkeys' number and power, he orders Mulplam to deal with the situation himself. Very disappointed that he has had no chance to slake his thirst for blood, Sahatsadecha marches all but a fraction of his army back to Longka.

146. *Mounted on woodland beasts, the monkeys charge Mulplam*

In the meantime, Hanuman has been rushing backwards and forwards through the wood, rallying the frightened monkeys. Now that Sahatsadecha has returned to Longka, the monkeys take heart and, under the lash of Hanuman's tongue, begin to filter back through the trees to open ground where they shamefacedly form up again behind their commanders. Indeed, Hanuman's efforts are so vigorous that not only are all the monkeys driven out of the wood but also most of the larger animals living there, so that the ranks of Ram's army are swelled by a curious assortment of wild beasts.

Hanuman is quick to see the possibilities of this situation. He mounts the eighteen generals on the backs of boars, sheep, buffaloes and bears, and leads them in a furious charge against the enemy. Mulplam's minions, accustomed to striking terror into the hearts of their enemy by virtue of their extraordinary composition and appearance, now sample a bitter draught of their own medicine.

147. *Phra Lak, aided by Hanuman, fights with Mulplam*

When the two sides have recoiled after the first furious onslaught, Mulplam orders his personal guard to isolate Phra Lak from his troops. He himself leads them in this maneuver, and when it has been successfully com-

142. *Two demon generals accompany Sahatsadecha*

141. *Sahatsadecha, with his concubines, rides out to battle*

144. *Two generals accompany Mulplam*   143. *Mulplam takes the field*

145. *Phra Ram and Phra Lak ride out to meet Sahatsadecha*

146. *Mounted on woodland beasts, the monkeys charge Mulplam*

pleted the commanders close on one another, shouting taunts and threats as they do so. Mulplam's hopes of a quick victory are dashed, though, for Hanuman sees what has happened and leads the eighteen royal generals to Lak's relief. While the battle rages around them, Lak and Mulplam dismount from their chariots and engage each other.

This personal combat between the Pangtan demon and the Prince of Ayutaya is closely contested, the demon thrusting and parrying with his deadly spear, Phra Lak countering with thunderous strokes of his great bow. How long this would have continued it is impossible to predict, but suddenly the monkey generals gain an advantage over the demon guard, and with a howl of triumph prepare to assist their leader. Mulplam sees that he must fly if he is to escape capture. Drawing back, he hurls his iron spear at Phra Lak, and, as he leaps into his chariot and makes off, he has the satisfaction of seeing his adversary sink to the ground, the spear protruding from his chest.

148. *Hanuman pulls the spear from Phra Lak's wound*

The monkey generals, horrified at this turn of events, gather round their fallen leader. While the others support him, Hanuman tries to withdraw the spear from his wound. For all his strength, however, he is unable to move it. Realizing that a spell has been cast over the weapon, Hanuman tries a little magic of his own. Laying his hands together, the Son of the Wind mutters three times a formula known only to himself. At the end of the third repetition, the spear falls from Phra Lak's body, the wound heals itself and Phra Lak rises up unharmed and ready to settle accounts with the demon leader. The monkey leaders return to their troops and the fighting once more becomes general.

149. *Mounted on Hanuman's shoulders, Phra Lak shoots at Mulplam*
150. *Phra Lak's arrow kills Mulplam*

Phra Lak's chariot has been damaged in the fighting, so Hanuman says another spell and enlarges himself. Taking Phra Lak on his shoulders, he leads him in search of the demon regent. Striking down hordes of demons, left and right, they fight their way over to Mulplam's chariot.

The first shaft that Phra Lak lets fly at Mulplam destroys his chariot and lays low his soldiers. Mulplam falls clear of the thrashing lions and hurls his discus at Lak. It hisses menacingly towards the prince, but with a sweep of his bow Phra Lak destroys it.

Mulplam is now without either weapons or troops. He leaps to his feet and, cursing the monkeys and their leaders, makes off as fast as he can go. Phra Lak lays another arrow to his bow, draws back, aiming carefully and lets the shaft loose. With lightning speed, the arrow strikes the demon's neck, killing him immediately. The monkeys let out a great cheer and then fall to searching for booty.

147. *Phra Lak, aided by Hanuman, fights with Mulplam*

148. *Hanuman pulls the spear from Phra Lak's wound*

231

150. *Phra Lak's arrow kills Mulplam*

149. *Mounted on Hanuman's shoulders, Phra Lak shoots at Mulplam*

As soon as the news of his brother's defeat reaches him in Longka, Sahatsadecha remusters his army and, swearing a terrible vengeance on the monkeys, marches it swiftly to the battlefield.

Pipeck, the wise demon, has told Phra Ram that this is exactly what the King of Pangtan will do. He warns Ram that Sahatsadecha is the possessor of a terrible club that kills whoever it is pointed against and advises the royal leader that Hanuman be sent to see what he can do to counter the threat of this weapon.

To undertake the mission, the Son of the Wind changes himself into a small white monkey, and leaves the camp to intercept Sahatsadecha. He has little time to wait. The demon has come up posthaste and after the outriders of his army have passed, Hanuman springs out of the undergrowth where he has been hiding directly into the path of the royal chariot. At this unexpected occurrence the lions pulling the chariot buck and shy and twist their traces, bringing the chariot, and indeed the whole army, to a halt. By this time Hanuman has leapt into a nearby tree, and the furious Sahatsadecha orders his soldiers to drag him down and put him to death.

"Don't kill me, great one," Hanuman whines, cringing and pretending to be terrified. "I've sought you out especially to put myself at your service. My one thought is the same as yours—to kill Phra Ram." And the ingenious monkey goes on to explain that he had been a citizen of Keetkin under Palee, but was made a slave when Phra Ram killed Palee and appointed Sukreep king in his place. From then on, he says, life has been unendurable for him, and he has escaped with the intention of killing Ram. He pleads with Sahatsadecha to be allowed to take part in the coming battle against the royal brothers.

The demon is rather taken with the idea of having a monkey in his service and permits Hanuman to sit on the shafts of his chariot. Then he orders his army to march on.

Well satisfied with this turn of affairs, Hanuman waits until the battlefield has been reached before making his next move. Then, when the two armies are confronting each other, he turns to Sahatsadecha, and trembling realistically, begs to be allowed to sit at the rear of the chariot, with the concubines.

"Pah, you monkeys are all cowards," says Sahatsadecha. But he is too preoccupied with the ordering of his forces to think of the danger of allowing a potential enemy to sit behind him, and says, "Go, do just as you wish."

Hanuman takes his position at the rear of the chariot. He casts an expert eye over the pleasure girls there—no situation is too urgent to inhibit thoughts of dalliance—and then, even as the demon army is breaking into the charge, mutters a spell to himself. He is immediately transformed into a giant monkey with four faces and eight arms, and so great is his weight that the chariot breaks to pieces beneath him, throwing Sahatsadecha and his concubines to the ground. Quick as a flash Hanuman seizes the demon's magic club. Even as the enraged Sahatsadecha is bellowing at his soldiers to kill the monkey, Hanuman points its deadly end at them, mowing them down like grass under the sickle. Having done so he breaks the club in two.

151. *Hanuman grapples with Sahatsadecha, who is trying to escape with his concubines*

Sahatsadecha now realizes the full danger of his position.   He snatches up his bow, meaning to kill Hanuman and make his escape, but the giant monkey tears it out of his hands like a toy from a child and throws it away. Exactly the same happens when the demon takes up his last weapon, a trident.   Disarmed and without a single soldier to support him, Sahatsadecha falls to his knees before Hanuman and begs for his life.

Hanuman, however, ignores his pleas.   He rolls the demon in his tail and brings him before Phra Ram.   The monkey soldiers, their terror at the first sight of this thousand-headed monster forgotten, now revile and taunt him and drag his concubines to watch his death agonies.   The demon pleads with each of his thousand tongues to be spared but Hanuman is unmoved.

"I shouldn't have thought death would have frightened a demon like you," he says flippantly.   "Besides, where you're going you'll be in good company, and you'd only be lonely here."   And with that, he takes up his trident and, to the applause of the monkeys, ends the life of the demon with one mighty blow.

With Sahatsadecha's concubines as the spoils of their victory, the monkey army returns triumphantly to camp.

152. *Hanuman kills Sahatsadecha*

THE DEATH OF TOTSAGAN
THE REUNION OF PHRA RAM AND NANG SEEDA

So desperate is Totsagan by this time that he takes his case to the heavenly court, feeling sure that as the matter is to be heard by his relative, Maleevarat the Just, the decision will be in his favor. The judge, however, decides the case on its merits, and orders the demon king to surrender Nang Seeda to her rightful husband. Totsagan returns to earth, determined to continue the war to its bitter end.

A series of battles follows. Although the fortunes of war are against Longka, and many demons and their allies are lost, Totsagan, without whose end all victories are hollow, appears to be invulnerable, and the most desperate efforts of the monkey army to kill him are without success.

So once more Phra Ram consults his demon seer. Pipeck tells him that Totsagan's soul is kept in a crystal casket which is guarded by a hermit, and that so long as this soul remains safe, the king of Longka himself cannot be killed. Hanuman at once offers to try to gain possession of it. The Son of the Wind seeks out the hermit, spins him a long and artful story, and succeeds in stealing the precious casket.

The problem now is to bring Totsagan to the field of battle, so that his soul and body may be destroyed simultaneously. The cunning monkey flies to the demon capital and there, prostrating himself before Totsagan, tells him that as his rewards for fighting for Phra Ram have been incommensurate with his services, he has now come to offer himself to the demons, hoping for better treatment. Completely taken in by this story, Totsagan welcomes Hanuman warmly and does all he can to bind him to Longka's cause, appointing him his heir to the kingdom and the holder of all the rights, titles and properties of his dead son Intorachit.

Genuinely delighted by these gifts—for they include the possession of the adorable Suwanna Kanyuma, Intorachit's widow—Hanuman leads the demon army against Phra Lak, and without inflicting any real damage on his brothers, manages to put the monkeys to flight and so cover himself with glory. On his return to the demon city, he is able to convince Totsagan that the final defeat of the humans and their cohorts is well within his grasp and persuades him to take part in the last battle in order to witness the downfall and death of his enemies.

When the two armies confront one another, Hanuman tells Totsagan that he will kill the royal brothers and fetch their bodies to him, and flying through the air comes to the chariot of Phra Ram. Prostrating himself before Ayutaya's royal exile, Hanuman shows him the casket containing Totsagan's soul, and tells him what he has achieved. Ram congratulates the monkey, and it is agreed that the demon shall be killed forthwith.

Hanuman places himself between the two armies. Holding the casket aloft, and spicing the information with many taunts and insults, Hanuman lets Totsagan know that he has been completely and finally deceived.

Even at this terrible moment, Totsagan adamantly refuses to give up Nang Seeda. He curses his enemy, telling him that if he fails to win her in this existence, then he will not fail to do so in the next. Assured that his situation is utterly without hope, he asks a favor of his adversary: that he shall be given one night of grace in which to take leave of Longka. The favor granted, Totsagan leads his army from the field and returns to his city.

Longka that night is a place of tears and lamentation. The demons know that their king must die in the morning, and they with him. Listlessly they take their last meals. Distractedly they seek the pleasure of their women. When these fail to annul the thoughts of the morrow, they seek oblivion in drink and sleep. Within the palace, Nang Monto pleads in vain with Totsagan to accept Phra Ram's terms. He tells her that death is preferable to a life stained by dishonor, and with that the subject is closed. The night passes.

The last morning dawns. Longka hums with activity as the demons arm themselves and muster for the battle. While the preparations are going forward, the demon king takes his farewell of the possessions that have given him such infinities of satisfaction. He walks through his palace of precious stones, the scene of so many of his finest occasions, looks into the chambers of gold where his life with his women and his children has passed. He continues to the gardens, where the dew still gleams from bud and flower, and knows that soon his eyes will be closed to such beauty. His thought returns to the cause of all his troubles, the incomparable Nang Seeda, and a shaft of pain, like the arrow he knows will soon end his life, penetrates his heart. At this moment the marshal arrives to tell him that the army is ready. Totsagan accepts the last tearful salutations of his ladies, climbs aboard his chariot and gives the order to advance. Clouds cover the sun, and the heavens thunder. The demon army leaves Longka.

Phra Ram's army is already drawn up on the battlefield, the heavenly bird Krut gliding above it, in readiness for the encounter. On seeing the enemy, the monkeys press forward, eager for the signal to attack. But before this is given, the commanders of the Ayutaya host have time to see that the demon captains are having the greatest difficulty in bringing their troops into position, for the demon soldiers are overcome with the terror of approaching death and want nothing more than to quit the field without conflict, leaving the monkeys victorious. Indeed, at every opportunity, demon soldiers melt into the woods adjoining the battlefield, while others, more accomplished, change themselves into birds and fly into the clouds. Phra Ram delays no longer. He gives the signal, and with a deep and terrifying howl, the monkey army launches itself into the attack.

It is in fact no battle at all, but a massacre. Demons, like dead leaves before the storm, fly here and there and fall in heaps upon the ground. Within minutes the only survivor of the carnage is Totsagan.

Proudly the King of Longka drives his chariot through the monkey ranks towards Phra Ram, and lets fly an arrow. It soars through the air with irresistible power, only to fall about Phra Ram at the last moment as a shower of blossoms. Seeing this, and observing that Phra Ram is fitting the Promat arrow to his bow, the demon tries his last ruse and assumes the form of Phra In. For a moment Phra Ram hesitates, but Hanuman, ever alert for such deceptions, urges him to shoot. Phra Ram lets the Promat arrow fly. Peals of thunder accompany its flight, and with the sound of mountains being torn asunder, the arrow buries itself in the breast of Totsagan, throwing him headlong to the ground, where he is seen in his true form once more—as the ten-headed, twenty-armed demon king.

His wound is mortal. Held in the arms of his brother Pipeck, he breathes out his last words, each of his ten mouths speaking in turn. The first accuses his brother of bringing about his downfall, but the others are conciliatory, instructing Pipeck to ascend the vacant throne of Longka, take on the possessions, rights and duties of the kingship, serve his people with justice and wisdom, and grant himself, Totsagan, the right to a royal cremation. Only the tenth mouth remains silent, for Hanuman sees the time has come and crushes to pieces the casket containing the demon's soul. At the moment of Totsagan's death, rejoicing is universal. The heavens resound to triumphal music, and the gods, giving way to their joy, dance and sing.

Only the ladies of Longka are silent. Within the empty city, they prepare for the royal funeral, weeping.

Held captive in the park beyond Longka's walls, Nang Seeda learns of her husband's victory only when Pipeck, at the head of a large retinue, comes to fetch her. Her heart trembles at the thought that she will soon come face to face with her lord, for almost fourteen years have passed since her abduction, and as she mounts the chariot that Pipeck places at her disposal, emotions almost too keen to bear trouble her breast.

At the sight of his lovely consort, Phra Ram, too, is torn by conflicting emotions. They greet each other with full formality, and Phra Ram then expresses the fear that has been tormenting him:

"Most beautiful Seeda, at last your elder brother is able to gladden his eyes with the form, more lovely than the moon, which has been absent from him for so long. This moment ends the heartache that he has borne in solitude for fourteen years—or perpetuates it for all time. For while your brother has suffered alone, you have been the captive and highest prize of the demon king."

At these words, and their allusion, Seeda covers her eyes and weeps that her fidelity can be doubted. But she soon recovers and demands to be put to the ordeal by fire. High in the Morot Mountains a site is chosen and a pyre built. Humans, monkeys, demons and even gods look on. A shaft from Ram's bow kindles the fire.

Nang Seeda sinks to her knees before her husband and lays her hands together. "The gods are my witness," she says, "that not Totsagan nor any man other than my own lord has known my love. If this is not the truth, may the flames devour me at the first step." Having paid her respects to the holy fire and Mother Earth, Seeda walks firmly into the pyre. With each footfall a lotus flower springs up, and the flames have no power to burn. Seeing this, the observers fall to their knees and the gods shower blessings upon Seeda.

As she steps from the flames, Phra Ram embraces Seeda, while that flower of womanhood clasps her husband's feet and assuages with copious tears the pain of fourteen years' parting.

Soon after this, the last rites are accorded the late king of Longka, and Pipeck accepts the crown from the hands of Phra Ram. The affairs of the demon island in order, the favorite of Isuan leads his army across to the mainland and back to Ayutaya. For his exile is now ended, and Phra Ram is king.

EPILOGUE

Under its new king, Ayutaya enjoyed many years of peace and prosperity. Beyond its walls, it is true, brief conflicts sprang to life, as demon survivors of the great conflict sought to regain their old power. But Ram had rewarded his allies generously on their disbanding and he had as little difficulty raising a fresh army to his banner as that army had in putting down the evil forces that opposed it, so it was never long before the commanders and their troops could disperse to their own realms once more—Sukreep and Ongkot to Keetkin, Chompoo to his kingdom of the same name, and Hanuman (now entitled Anuchit) to his own city of Nopburi.

But scattered though the demons were, they continued to nurture an implacable hostility towards Ayutaya, and it was one of their number who contrived the final breach between Phra Ram and Nang Seeda.

It happened in this way. A distant relative of Totsagan, Adoon by name, decided to see what mischief she could cause in Ayutaya as revenge for her king's defeat. Disguising herself as a pretty girl of good family, she inveigled herself into the position of maid of honor to Nang Seeda. One day, pretending to be curiosu to know what her captor had looked like, Adoon persuaded Nang Seeda to make a sketch of the demon. No sooner had this been done than Adoon reassumed her true form, laid a curse on the slate and disappeared. To her horror, Nang Seeda found that no matter how hard she tried, she could not erase the image, and, thoroughly frightened, she hid the slate, hoping it would never come to light. This was not to be. The slate caused a fire within the palace and was quickly brought to Phra Ram's attention. The king's fury at what he first thought was a wretched joke was intensified beyond all bounds when he learned the true facts, and imagining that Seeda had after all deceived him with the demon king, he ordered Phra Lak to take her to the forest and there put her to death.

Nang Seeda, who sought nothing more than a quick and merciful end if she were to be the object of her husband's suspicion, commanded the reluctant Phra Lak to kill her without delay. But the gods intervened, and the moment that the sword touched her neck it was transformed into a garland of flowers. Seeing how the matter stood, Lak left Seeda in the forest, commending her to the continued protection of the gods, and returned to Ayutaya with the heart of a deer, which he showed to Phra Ram as evidence that he had carried out his order.

At the time of these happenings, Nang Seeda had been three months pregnant, and in due course, under the care of the friendly hermit Watchamarik, she gave birth to a boy, whom she named Mongkot. Watchamarik, exercising his magic arts, created a companion for the royal child, and the two grew up happily together, learning much and acquiring great powers from the hermit.

So remarkable were the feats the boys were able to perform that Phra Ram himself heard of them, and fearing that they posed a threat to the safety of the kingdom, ordered that they should be captured and imprisoned. As no one else proved capable of carrying out his command, he tried to capture the boys himself, and in the process learned the true parentage of Mongkot. The intervening years had been more than sufficient for him to learn to deplore his suspicions of Nang Seeda, and he wished nothing better than that she should forgive him and return to Ayutaya with her children to reign once more as his queen. But Seeda's love was by now mingled with resentment at her former treatment, and the fear that Ram's suspicion might again be aroused by his jealousy. Recognizing his right to bring up their son, however, she permitted the two boys to go back to Ayutaya with the king.

Phra Ram now bent his efforts to persuading his wife to return to him. When these all failed, he resorted to a trick. He had the news carried to her that he had died, and when she came to weep at his urn, as he had foreseen she would, he tried to detain her in the city against her will. This proved an unwise action, for Seeda appealed to Mother Earth for protection, and was immediately carried off to the subterranean realm of the snake king, Wiroon Nakarat. And there, for some years, the matter rested.

The gods, of course, had been following this unhappy affair with some interest and—towards the end—a certain impatience. Eventually, after convening a heavenly council, Phra Isuan sent to the underworld for Nang Seeda and demanded to know of her why, when the whole world was living in happiness and harmony, she alone continued to prosecute her feud against her husband. Having heard her side of the case, Phra Isuan sent for his protégé to learn what he had to say for himself. When Phra Ram had spoken, the gods deliberated.

It was Phra Isuan, as the god most closely concerned with the conflict from its inception, who passed judgement. He chided Phra Ram for his mistrust, which he pointed out was utterly misplaced. Nang Seeda he upbraided for her foolishness in being deceived by the demon Adoon. He censured, too, her obstinacy, which he considered had been carried beyond the point to which a wife might venture in punishing an errant husband. And in conclusion he commanded that the quarrel be brought to an immediate end and the couple reunite.

Phra Ram could not have asked for a more pleasing verdict. As for Nang Seeda, if any latent rebelliousness still smouldered in her breast, she masked it, for who in their proper senses dare disobey the gods? To set the seal on the reconciliation, the couple were honored with a banquet in the holy palace atop Mount Krailat, in the course of which they reaffirmed their marriage vows. And then, while the heavens sang and the earth danced, Phra Ram and Nang Seeda were borne back to Ayutaya aboard Phra In's diamond chariot, and there they spent the rest of their long and honorable lives—presumably in perfect amity, for if any other storms disturbed their marital bliss, they passed unknown alike to gods and men.

DRAMATIS PERSONAE

BIBLIOGRAPHY

INDEX

DRAMATIS PERSONAE

(Since the principal characters appear very frequently, only the number of the panel in which they first appear is given.)

Ayutaya Humans

Phra Ram — Exiled King of Ayutaya, incarnation of the god Narai. Recognizable by stylized human face (Panel 1). When he reverts to divine form he is pictured with four arms (Panel 6).

Phra Lak — Brother of Ram, incarnation of snake god Ananta Nakarat. In appearance identical to Ram. In panels where they appear together, Lak is always in an inferior (lower) position (Panel 1).

Nang Seeda — Ram's wife, incarnation of the goddess Lakshmi. Daughter of Totsagan and Nang Monto. Distinguishable from male humans mainly by partial exposure of breasts. Indistinguishable from female demons, except that on the rare occasions when they are pictured together (Panel 72), she is in superior position.

Allies of Ayutaya

Hanuman — Son of the Wind, a monkey with great magical powers. As with all the monkeys, distinguishable from the demons by a kind of circular cheek pouch. Always shown without headdress (Panel 4).

Palee; *Sukreep*	Sons of the god In and the Sun respectively, and Hanuman's uncles. King and regent respectively of Keetkin city until Palee's death, when Sukreep succeeds to the throne. Both wear headdresses with conical peaks with a spur (Panel 5).
Ongkot	Son of Palee and Nang Monto. His headdress is topped by a bladelike peak (Panel 5).

Dara	Wife successively of Palee and Sukreep. Does not appear in panels.
Chompoo	Monkey king of Chompoo City. Not identifiable.
Chompooparn	A friend of Hanuman. Appears in panel 9.
Pipeck	Demon brother of Totsagan. Easy to recognize as the only demon in the Ayutaya camp (Panel 51).
Nilek	Monkey general (Panel 53).
Nilapat	Foster son of Chompoo. Similar in appearance to Hanuman (Panel 78).
Prakontan	A spirit. To be distinguished from monkeys by sharper nose and rounder eyes (Panels 95 and 98).

A Hermit

Nart	Human being. Hermit's hat and beard (Panel 18).

Beasts and Birds

Sadayu	Great bird, friendly to Ayutaya (Panel 3).
Sampatee	Elder brother of Sadayu (Panel 16).
Krut	Heavenly bird. Enemy of snakes (Panel 123).
Matchanu	Son of Hanuman and Supanna Matcha, with monkey body and fish tail (Panel 109).

Divine Ladies

Butsa Malee Protectress of the city of Mayan. Identical to all other ladies, except for minor differences in headdress (Panels 14, 15).

Suwanna Malee Sister of Butsa Malee. Does not appear in panels.

Supanna Matcha Daughter of Totsagan and sea goddess. Mother of Matchanu. Head and torso of woman, with tail of fish (Panels 91, 92).

Longka Demons

Totsagan King of Longka, incarnation of Nontok, a divine courtier. Wears headdress with many faces (Panel 2).

Nang Monto Totsagan's wife. Heavenly beauty given to Totsagan by Isuan. Appearance identical to Nang Seeda and all other divine ladies and female demons except for minor differences in headdress (Panel 24).

Intorachit Son of Totsagan and Monto. Similar facially to other demons. Wears headdress with conical peak and spur (Panel 33).

Suwanna Kanyuma Wife of Intorachit. Appearance as for other female demons (Panel 43).

Kumpagan Regent of Longka, brother of Totsagan. No headdress (Panel 44).

Samanaka Sister of Totsagan. Does not appear.

Nonyawik; Waiyuwake Nephews of Totsagan. Wearing what appear to be small turbans (Panels 103 and 104).

Pan Sahatsa Kuman One thousand sons of Totsagan, each with seven faces. Three shown being killed by Hanuman in panel 32.

Dreechada	Wife of Pipeck. Probably shown in panel 43, certainly in panel 71.
Benyagai	Daughter of Pipeck and Dreechada. Identical to other female demons and divine ladies (Panel 69).
Wirunyamuk	A demon general. Wears small turban (Panels 126–128).
Sukrasan	A demon courtier (Panels 63, 64 and 67, 68).
Mareet	A demon courtier. Appears only in panel 1, as the dead gazelle on Phra Ram's back.

ALLIES OF LONGKA

Maiyarap	Demon Lord of the Underworld. Appears in panels 104, 105, 108, 111 and 112, wearing a headdress with flamelike peak. In panel 106 he wears the robes and turban of a hermit.
Jantraprapa	Mother of Maiyarap (Panel 105).
Pirakuan	Sister of Maiyarap (Panel 110).
Waiyawik	Son of Pirakuan. Does not appear.
Sahatsadecha	King of Pangtan. Demon with one thousand heads and therefore shown wearing many-faced headdress, identical to Totsagan. Appears only once (Panel 137) with King of Longka, and then in inferior position. In panels 141, 151 and 152 is easily identified.
Mulplam	Brother of Sahatsadecha. Wavy-haired, no headdress other than circlet of gold and jewels (Panels 137, 143, 147 and 150).

GODS

Phra Isuan *Phra Prom* *Phra Narai*	Heavenly gods, listed in approximate order of importance and power. Narai appears as Ram, with four arms holding bow, conch, discus and trident. Witsanukam is shown

Phra Witsanukam	holding conch, and In holding sword, in panel 49. Phra
Phra In	Prom and Isuan do not appear.

ELEMENTS

Phra Artit	The Sun, father of Sukreep
Phra Pai	Wind God, father of Hanuman
Phra Piroon	Rain God. None of these elements appears.

MONSTERS

Baklan	In appearance identical to a demon (Panels 11, 12 and 13).
Panurat	As for Baklan (Panels 96, 97).
Pee Sua Samut	A female monster, guarding the strait of Longka (Panel 17 only).

BIBLIOGRAPHY

SOUTHEAST ASIA AND THAILAND

Benedict, Ruth. "Thai Culture and Behavior." Unpublished wartime study, Sept., 1943; data paper no. 4, Southeast Asia Program. New York: Cornell Univ. Reprinted 1952.

Coedes, George. *Pour Mieux Comprendre Angkor*. Maisonneuve, 1947.

Chakrabongse, Prince Chula. *Lords of Life*. London: Alvin Redman, 1960.

Diskul, Subhadradis. *Ayudhia Art*. Bangkok, 1956.

Hall, D.G.E. *History of Southeast Asia*. London: Macmillan, 1955.

Insor, D. *Thailand*. New York: Praeger, 1963.

May, R.le. *A Concise History of Buddhist Art in Siam*. Cambridge, 1938.

.... *The Culture of Southeast Asia*. London: Allen and Unwin, 1954.

Rawson, Phillip. *The Art of Southeast Asia*. London: Thames and Hudson, 1967.

Turpin, M. *History of the Kingdom of Siam*. Bangkok: American Presbyterian Missionary Press, 1908.

Vella, Walter. *Siam under Rama III*. New York: J.J. Augostin, 1957.

Wales, H.G. *Siamese State Ceremonies*. London: B. Quaritch, 1931.

.... *The Making of Greater India*. London: B. Quaritch.

Wood, W.A.R. *History of Siam*. Bangkok: Chalermnit, 1924.

THE RAMAYANA

Frazer, R.W. *Literary History of India*. London: Fisher Unwin, 1898.

Gurage, Ananda. *The Society of the Ramayana*. Ceylon: Saman Press, 1960.

Sister Nivedata. *Myths of the Hindus*. London: Harrap, 1913.

Valmiki (M.N. Dutt, ed.) *Ramayana*. Calcutta: Chakravarti, 1963.

Wilkins, W.J. *Hindu Mythology*. London: Thacker & Co., 1882.

Wilson, E.P. *Hindu Literature*. London: Colonial Press, 1900.

THE RAMAKIEN

Swami Satyananda Puri and Charoen Sarahiran. *The Ramakirti.*[1] Bangkok: Dharmashrama.
The Thai Ramayana.[2] Bangkok: Chalermnit.
Velder, C. *Kampf der Goetter und Daemonen.* Schweinfurt: Verlag Neues Forum, 1962.
Olsson, Ray. A. *Translation of Kampf der Goetter und Daemonen.* Bangkok: Praepitaya Co. Ltd., 1968.

[1] A narration of the central episode, in curious English, long out of print.
[2] A bald summary in bad English; unreliable.

SOURCES IN THE THAI LANGUAGE

(NOTE: *It is extremely difficult to compile a complete bibliography of Thai books since the name of the publisher and the dates are seldom included in the book.*)

Rama I. *Ramakien.* Bangkok: Klangwitya.
Rama II. *Ramakien.* Bangkok: Klangwitya.
Tongnoi, Pikoon. *Ramakien* (prose summary of Rama I's *Ramakien*).
Sathien Koset and Nakaratit. *Ramakien Characters.*
Phrya Anuman Rajathon. *Ramakien Characters in Lakon.*

INDEX